FASHION ILLUSTRATIONS 2

グラフィック社

FASHION ILUSTRATIONS 2

Expressing Textures

by Kojiro Kumagai
Copyright © 1988 by Graphic-sha Publishing Co., Ltd.
1-9-12 Kudan-Kita, Chiyoda-ku, Tokyo, Japan
ISBN 4-7661-0483-8

はじめに

ファッションデザイナーのプロの方や，これからプロをめざして勉強をしている方，ファッションコーディネーター，スタイリスト，イラストレーター，趣味でイラストを描いている方達の中で，ファッション画や人物画の形は描けても，いざ色を塗り始めたら，その塗り方や，どんな画材をどのように使えばいいのか，素材感を出すにはどうすればいいのか分からないことがたくさんあって苦労しているなどということをよく聞きます。

そんな悩みをお持ちの方のために，本書では，いろいろな画材（水彩，パステル，マーカー等）での色の塗り方，柄（ストライプ，チェック，ヘリンボーン等）の描き方，素材感（毛皮，デニム，ニット，ラメ，ベルベット等）の描き方を，多数の作品を載せて編集しました。

色の塗り方や，素材感を出す描き方が上手になるためには，できるだけたくさんの作品を描く以外に方法はないでしょう。

上手に描くことが出来るようになれば，自然に感性も磨かれてくるはずです。楽しみながら描き続け，いろいろなテクニックを自分のものにしましょう。

Prologue:

It is not unusual for professional fashion designers, students working towards this goal, fashion coordinators, stylists, illustrators, and even those who like to design clothes just for fun to be able to accurately draw the figure and design. However, when it comes to actually adding color, it is often difficult to select the correct method, and to express the fabric's texture and unique qualities. In order to assist such people in their goal towards the perfect illustration, we have selected a variety of methods (water colors, pastels, markers, etc.), patterns (stripes, checks, herringbones, etc.), and fabrics (fur, denim, knits, lamé, velvet, etc.) to introduce, to the reader. It is our belief that the only to learn to accurately portray these is to practice drawing as many illustrations as possible. Once this is accomplished, a certain sensitivity will naturally develop. It is important to enjoy what you are doing, and have fun while acquiring the different techniques introduced here.

目　次
Contents

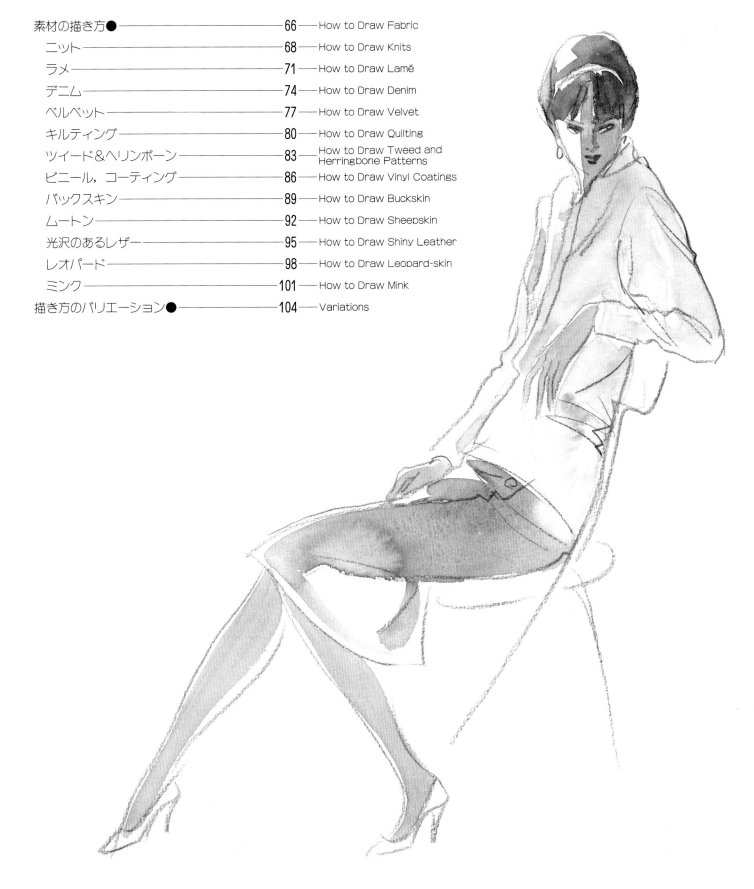

現代はファッションの時代である。コスチュームからヘアスタイルはもちろんのこと，車，インテリア，日常生活の器具，グルメに至るまで現代人の衣・食・住の主要な生活分野すべてがファッションによって支配されているといえるでしょう。

それぞれのスタイルが変化する時，新しいファッションが生み出され，そのファッションを創造し，あるいは伝達するのがイラストレーションの分野です。

ファッションに感心を示し，あれこれとアイデアを考えることは，大変楽しいことです。ディテールの発想やアイデアがいくら良くても，全体のシルエットやバランス，色の組み合わせなどをいくら頭の中でまとめようとしても，なかなかまとまらないものですし，また瞬間に浮んだアイデアはすぐに忘れてしまうものです。そのような時にメモをし描くことによって，新たなアイデアが偶然生まれることもあります。

ファッションデザイナーの仕事は，アイデアを相手に伝達しなければなりません。自分の描いたファッションイラスト表現が正確に相手に伝わらなければ，プロのデザイナーとしては失格です。

また，ファッションイラストレーションでも表現方法は，用途によっていろいろな描き方があります。ファッションメーカーのデザイナーの描き方，学生がデザインコンクールに出品するための描き方，プロのデザイナーとしての描き方，ユニホームデザインのユニホームイラストの描き方，プロのファッションイラストレーターとしての描き方など，さまざまなテクニック表現がありますが，どんな表現方法にも共通して言えることは，デザイン，シルエット，全体のデザインバランス，丈のバランス，ディテールの位置，大きさなどの自分のデザインの意図が正確に相手に伝達されることです。

これから，デザイナーやファッションイラストレーターになろうとしている方達は，まずこれらのイラスト表現が正確でなければ，プロとしての仕事は出来ないと言えるでしょう。

It can be said that we have entered the "Era of Fashion." Not only does fashion play an extremely important role in the clothes that we wear and the hair-styles that we choose, but also in the many other aspects of our daily lives, such as cars, interiors, and food. Each time a particular style changes, and new fashions are born, is the role of the illustrator to create and express these new ideas.

Having an interest in fashion and creating new ideas can be very exciting and rewarding. However, simply having a concept, no matter how excellent and detailed it may be, is not sufficient. It is difficult to actually visualize the overall silhouette, balance, and combination of colors without putting it down on paper. It is not unusual to suddenly have an inspiration by doing so, either.

It is the fashion designer's goal to relate an idea to another individual or group of individuals. Unless this is successfully accomplished, you will fall as a professional designer. Moreover, it must be understood that there are a variety of ways to express fashion illustrations, depending on the particular purpose of the design. The technique will differ according to the goal, whether it be that of a designer working for a fashion maker, a student submitting his/her work to a design contest, a professional designer, a uniform designer, or a professional fashion illustrator. The one thing common to all of the above, however, is that the idea must accurately be related to the viewer, in regards to the silhouette, the overall balance, the hem-line's balance, the positioning of details, and general scale.

For those of you who are seriously considering a career as a designer or fashion illustrator, it is essential to remember the above points, and to be able to accurately express your ideas through illustrations.

ファッション
イラストレーションの描き方

顔，ヘアの描き方／
人体プロポーション／
美しく見えるポーズ／
画材と用具／
プロポーション肉付け／着装／
コスチューム部分練習／
ディフォルメの描き方／
デザインシルエット／
コスチュームパターン

HOW TO DRAW FASHION
ILLUSTRATIONS

Drawing the Face and Hair/
Human Body Proportions/
Attractive Poses/
Materials and Tools/
Contouring the Body/Dressing (Adding the Costume)
Practice for Individual Costume Parts/
Drawing with Deformation/
Design Silhouettes/
Costume   Patterns/

顔の描き方プロポーション
Correct Proportions for Drawing Faces

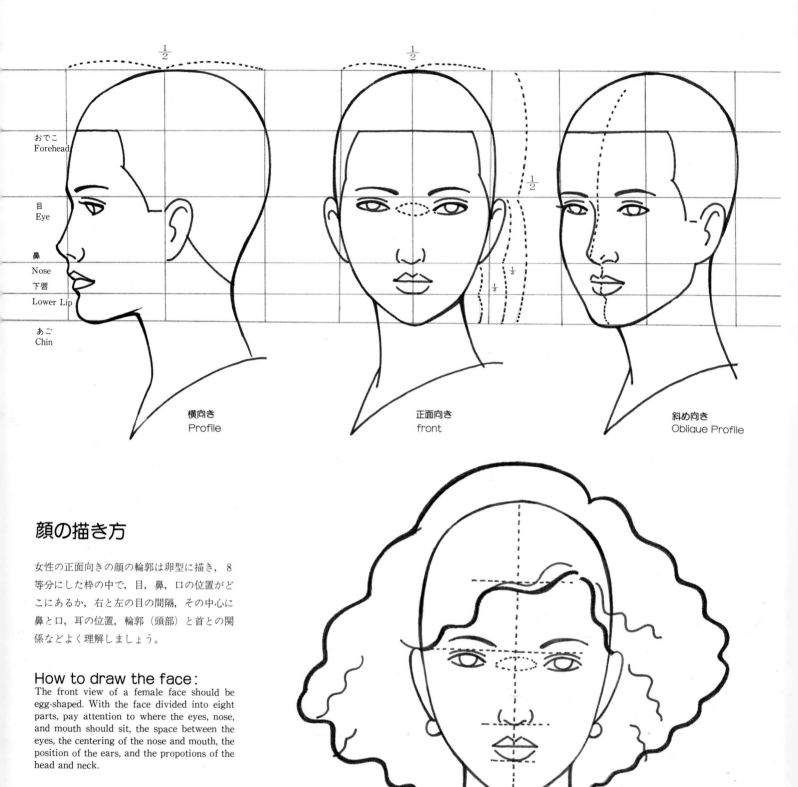

おでこ
Forehead

目
Eye

鼻
Nose

下唇
Lower Lip

あご
Chin

横向き
Profile

正面向き
front

斜め向き
Oblique Profile

顔の描き方

女性の正面向きの顔の輪郭は卵型に描き，8
等分にした枠の中で，目，鼻，口の位置がど
こにあるか，右と左の目の間隔，その中心に
鼻と口，耳の位置，輪郭（頭部）と首との関
係などよく理解しましょう。

How to draw the face:

The front view of a female face should be
egg-shaped. With the face divided into eight
parts, pay attention to where the eyes, nose,
and mouth should sit, the space between the
eyes, the centering of the nose and mouth, the
position of the ears, and the propotions of the
head and neck.

ヘアの描き方

ヘアスタイルを描くとき，頭頂，前・横・後の各部分の
髪の流れをひとつの固りとして大まかにとらえ，頭の輪
郭よりも大きく描きます。
また，髪の流れはどんなスタイルでもS字型やL字型に
流れ，直線の流れはありません。

How to draw hair :

When drawing hair, capture the general style, illustrating
the top, front, side, and back in one flow. Make sure that
the hair's outline is drawn larger than that of the head.
It is also important to remember that hair should always
be illustrated in "S" or "L" shapes, and never in straight
lines.

9

顔の描き方応用
Applications for drawing faces

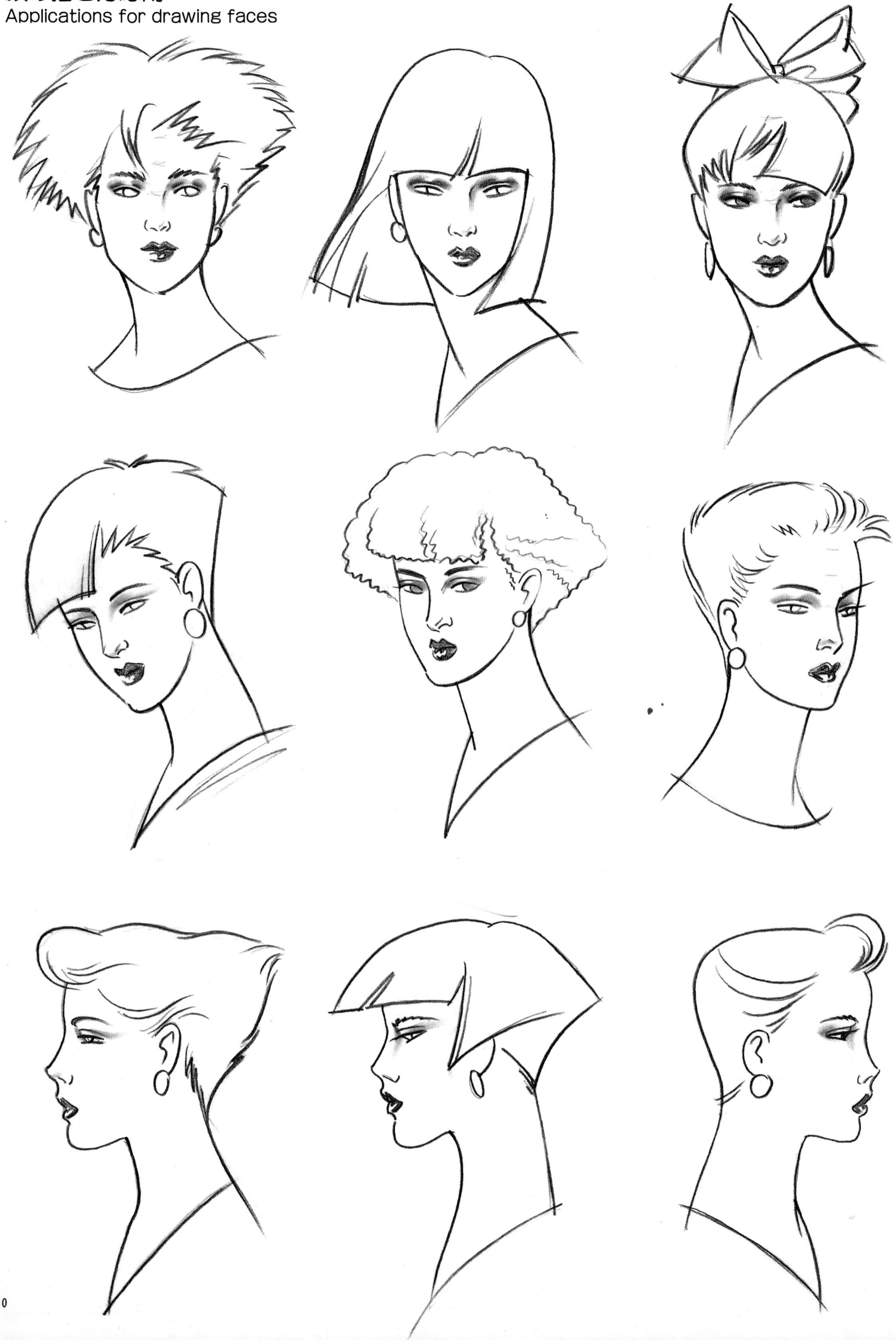

自分で顔のいろいろなポーズを省略的に描いて練習しましょう。
Practice drawing simplified versions of different angles and poses of the human face.

人体プロポーション
Correct Proportions of the Human Body

正面向き8頭身プロポーション
Front View of 1 : 8 Proportion

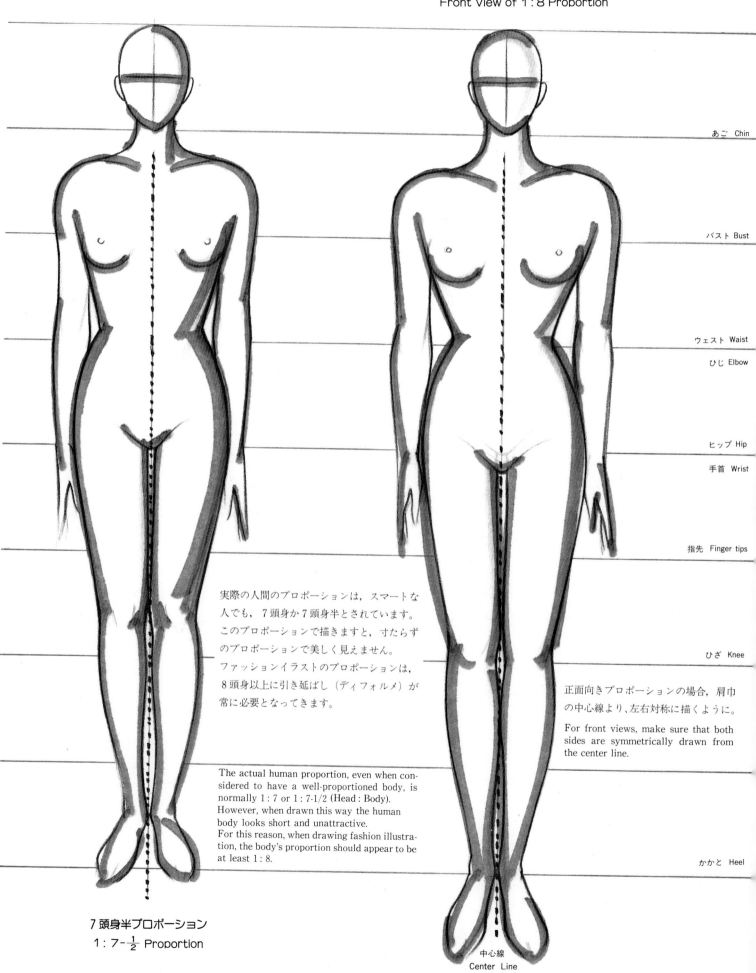

あご　Chin

バスト　Bust

ウェスト　Waist

ひじ　Elbow

ヒップ　Hip

手首　Wrist

指先　Finger tips

ひざ　Knee

かかと　Heel

実際の人間のプロポーションは，スマートな
人でも，7頭身か7頭身半とされています。
このプロポーションで描きますと，寸たらず
のプロポーションで美しく見えません。
ファッションイラストのプロポーションは，
8頭身以上に引き延ばし（ディフォルメ）が
常に必要となってきます。

正面向きプロポーションの場合，肩巾
の中心線より、左右対称に描くように。

For front views, make sure that both
sides are symmetrically drawn from
the center line.

The actual human proportion, even when con-
sidered to have a well-proportioned body, is
normally 1 : 7 or 1 : 7-1/2 (Head : Body).
However, when drawn this way the human
body looks short and unattractive.
For this reason, when drawing fashion illustration, the body's proportion should appear to be
at least 1 : 8.

7頭身半プロポーション
1 : 7-$\frac{1}{2}$ Proportion

中心線
Center Line

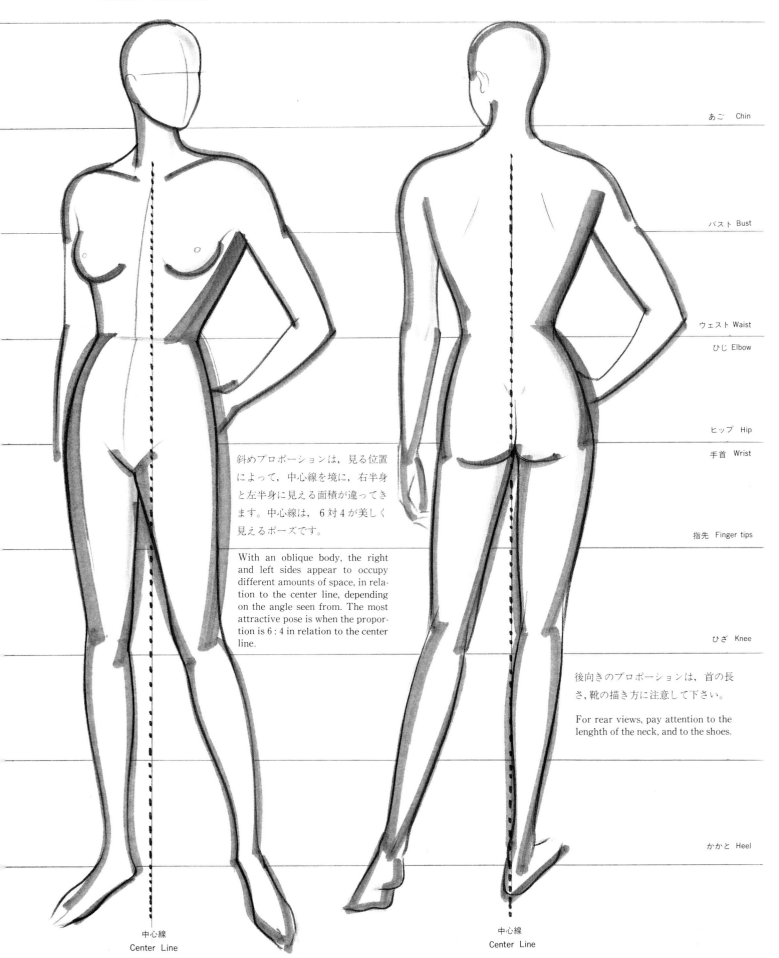

斜め向き8頭身プロポーション
Oblique 1：8 Proportion

後向き8頭身プロポーション
Rear 1：8 Proportion

あご　Chin

バスト Bust

ウェスト Waist

ひじ Elbow

ヒップ Hip

手首 Wrist

指先 Finger tips

ひざ Knee

かかと Heel

斜めプロポーションは，見る位置
によって，中心線を境に，右半身
と左半身に見える面積が違ってき
ます。中心線は，6対4が美しく
見えるポーズです。

With an oblique body, the right
and left sides appear to occupy
different amounts of space, in relation to the center line, depending
on the angle seen from. The most
attractive pose is when the proportion is 6：4 in relation to the center
line.

後向きのプロポーションは，首の長
さ，靴の描き方に注意して下さい。

For rear views, pay attention to the
lenght of the neck, and to the shoes.

中心線
Center Line

中心線
Center Line

13

美しく見えるポーズ

ファッションイラストを描くときに大切な課題にポーズの研究があります。コスチュームデザインの美しさは，ポーズの美しさによって表現されると言っても過言ではありません。

Attractive Poses

An important topic when drawing fashion illustration is the study of different poses. It can even be said that the attractiveness of the costume design depends on that of the pose.

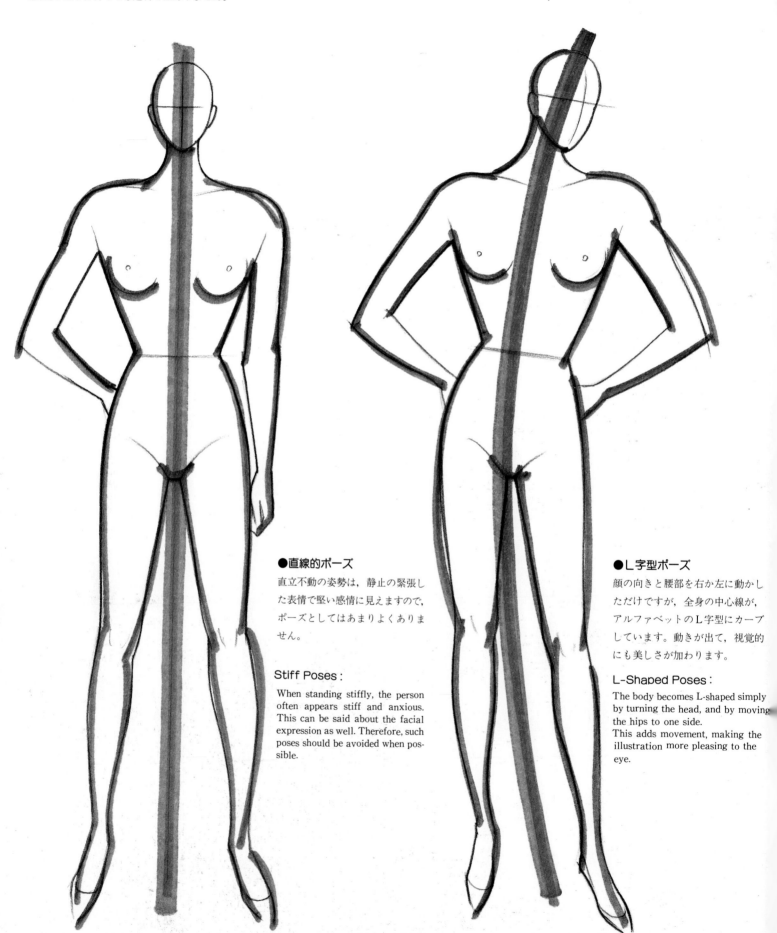

●直線的ポーズ

直立不動の姿勢は，静止の緊張した表情で堅い感情に見えますので，ポーズとしてはあまりよくありません。

Stiff Poses:

When standing stiffly, the person often appears stiff and anxious. This can be said about the facial expression as well. Therefore, such poses should be avoided when possible.

●L字型ポーズ

顔の向きと腰部を右か左に動かしただけですが，全身の中心線が，アルファベットのL字型にカーブしています。動きが出て，視覚的にも美しさが加わります。

L-Shaped Poses:

The body becomes L-shaped simply by turning the head, and by moving the hips to one side.
This adds movement, making the illustration more pleasing to the eye.

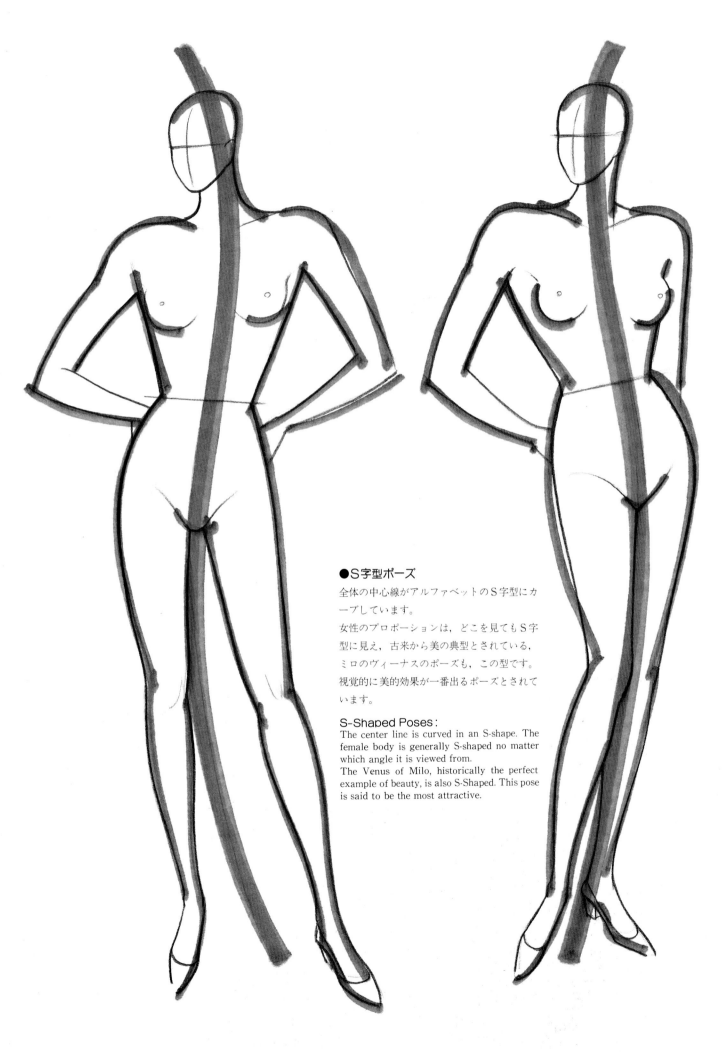

●S字型ポーズ

全体の中心線がアルファベットのS字型にカーブしています。

女性のプロポーションは，どこを見てもS字型に見え，古来から美の典型とされている，ミロのヴィーナスのポーズも，この型です。

視覚的に美的効果が一番出るポーズとされています。

S-Shaped Poses:

The center line is curved in an S-shape. The female body is generally S-shaped no matter which angle it is viewed from.

The Venus of Milo, historically the perfect example of beauty, is also S-Shaped. This pose is said to be the most attractive.

重心の軸脚

立ちポーズの時に一番大切なことは，重心のかかっている軸脚がどの位置にあるかということです。
腰が出ている方に重心が移動するので，重心がかかっている脚がかならず軸脚になります。その時には，首の中心線の直下に軸脚のかかとが近くに来ます。
なお，軸脚よりも遊脚を少し長目に描いた方が，脚がスマートに長く見えます。

Axial Leg:

The most important point to remember with standing positions is where the supporting leg is located. Since gravity is naturally shifted to the side which the hips move to, this side always becomes the axial leg. In this case, The heel of the axial foot should be drawn close to the neck's center line. Also, remember that the non-axial leg should be drawn longer than the axial leg to make the legs appear longer and more attractive.

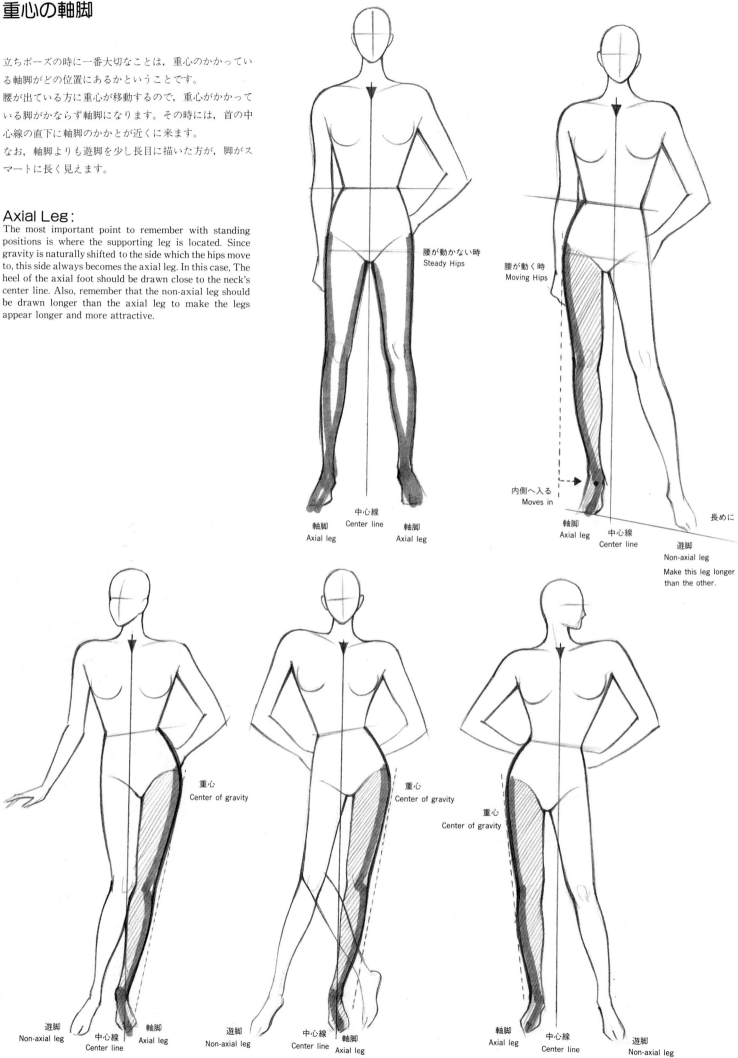

腰が動かない時
Steady Hips

中心線
Center line

軸脚
Axial leg

軸脚
Axial leg

腰が動く時
Moving Hips

内側へ入る
Moves in

軸脚
Axial leg

中心線
Center line

遊脚
Non-axial leg

長めに

Make this leg longer than the other.

重心
Center of gravity

遊脚
Non-axial leg

中心線
Center line

軸脚
Axial leg

重心
Center of gravity

遊脚
Non-axial leg

中心線
Center line

軸脚
Axial leg

重心
Center of gravity

軸脚
Axial leg

中心線
Center line

遊脚
Non-axial leg

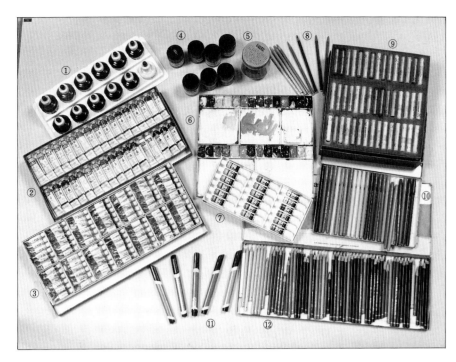

1. カラーインク
2. リキテックス
3. 水彩
4. ポスターカラー（ビン）
5. リキテックス・マットバニッシュ
6. パレット
7. ポスターカラー（チューブ）
8. パステル鉛筆
9. パステル（ソフトタイプ）
10. マービーマーカー
11. パントーンマーカー
12. 色鉛筆

1. Conlored Ink
2. Liquitex
3. Water Colors
4. Poster Colors (Bottle)
5. Liquitex/Matte Varnish
6. Palette
7. Poster Colors (Tube)
8. Pastel Pencils
9. Pastels (Soft Type)
10. Marvy Marker
11. Pantone Marker
12. Colored Pencils

1. 溶き皿
2. パレット
3. 筆洗
4. ドライヤー
5. ぼかし網
6. ぼかし刷毛
7. 歯ブラシ
8. 筆類
9. デザインカッター
10. カッター
11. サインペン
12. 芯研器
13. 鉛筆削り
14. 修正液
15. 消しゴム類
16. 製図用インク
17. 擦筆
18. ペン
19. 鉛筆

1. Mixing/Dissolving Plate
2. Palette
3. Container for Cleaning Brushes
4. Dryer
5. Vignetting Net
6. Vignetting Brush
7. Toothbrush
8. Brushes
9. Design Cutter (Knife)
10. Cutter (Knife)
11. Felt-tip Pens
12. Lead Sharpener
13. Pencil Sharpener
14. Correction Fluid
15. Erasers
16. Drafting Ink
17. Stumps
18. Pens
19. Pencils

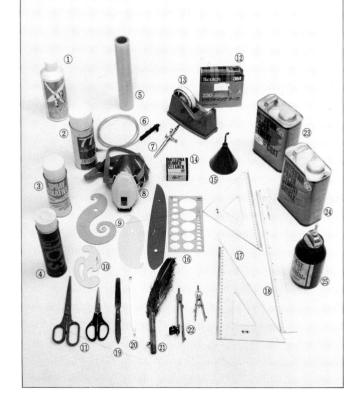

1. エアーボンベ
2. スプレーのり
3. フィキサチーフ
4. レトラコート
5. マスキングシート
6. レトラジェット
7. ハンドピース
8. 防塵マスク
9. ユニカーブ
10. 雲形定規
11. ハサミ
12. ドラフティングテープ
13. セロハンテープ
14. ラバークリーナー
15. ディスペンサー
16. 円定規
17. 三角定規
18. 直定規
19. パレットナイフ
20. ガラス棒
21. 羽ボウキ
22. コンパス
23. ペーパーセメント
24. ソルベックス
25. セメントディスペンサー

1. Air Cylinder
2. Spray Glue
3. Fixative
4. Letracote
5. Masking Sheet
6. Letra Jet
7. Hand Piece
8. Mask
9. Uni-Curve
10. French Curves
11. Scissors
12. Drafting Tape
13. Scotch Tape
14. Rubber Cleaner
15. Dispenser
16. Templet
17. Triangle
18. Ruler
19. Palette Knife
20. Glass Rod
21. Feather Brush
22. Compass
23. Paper Cement
24. Solvex
25. Cement Dispenser

正面向きプロポーション肉付け
Proportion

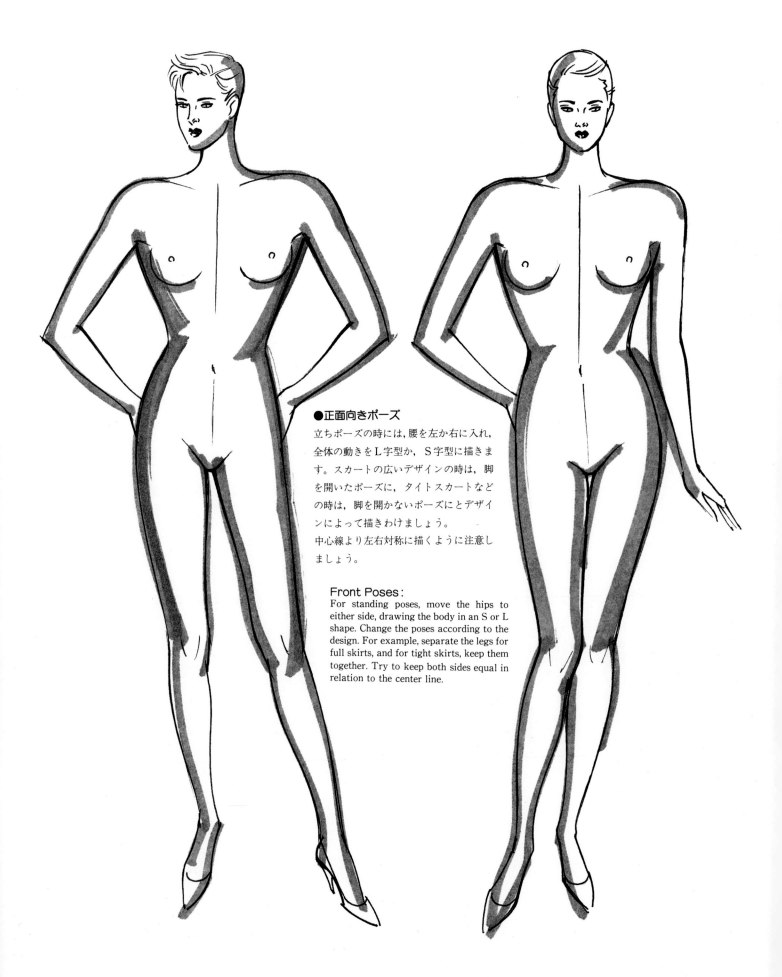

●正面向きポーズ

立ちポーズの時には，腰を左か右に入れ，
全体の動きをL字型か，S字型に描きま
す。スカートの広いデザインの時は，脚
を開いたポーズに，タイトスカートなど
の時は，脚を開かないポーズにとデザイ
ンによって描きわけましょう。
中心線より左右対称に描くように注意し
ましょう。

Front Poses :

For standing poses, move the hips to
either side, drawing the body in an S or L
shape. Change the poses according to the
design. For example, separate the legs for
full skirts, and for tight skirts, keep them
together. Try to keep both sides equal in
relation to the center line.

斜め向きプロポーション肉付け
Proportion

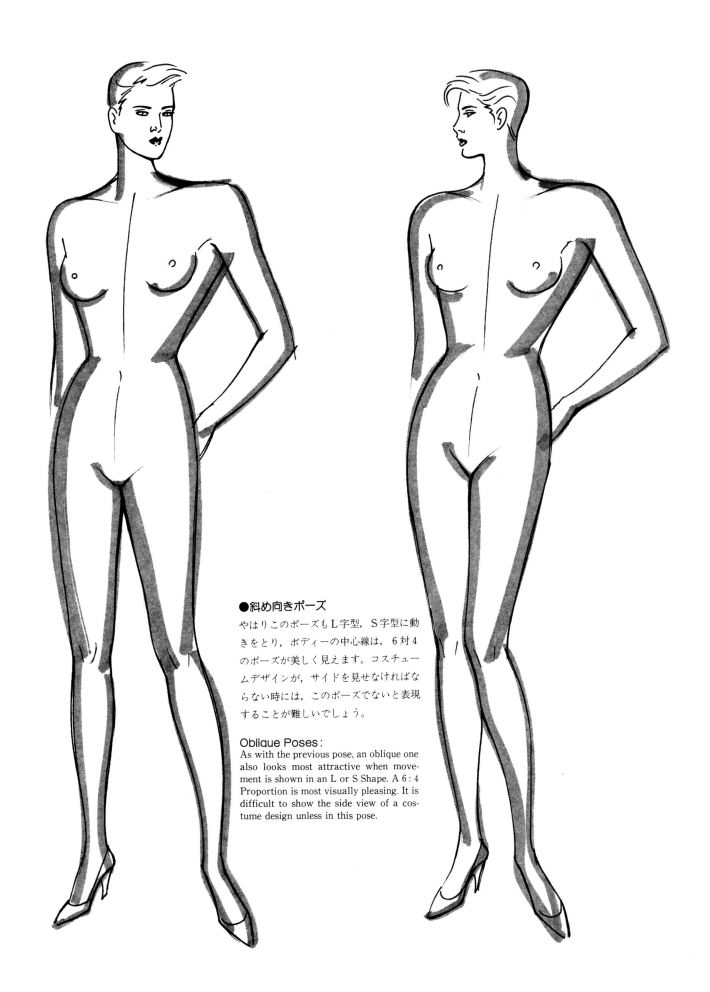

●斜め向きポーズ

やはりこのポーズもL字型，S字型に動きをとり，ボディーの中心線は，6対4のポーズが美しく見えます。コスチュームデザインが，サイドを見せなければならない時には，このポーズでないと表現することが難しいでしょう。

Oblique Poses:

As with the previous pose, an oblique one also looks most attractive when movement is shown in an L or S Shape. A 6 : 4 Proportion is most visually pleasing. It is difficult to show the side view of a costume design unless in this pose.

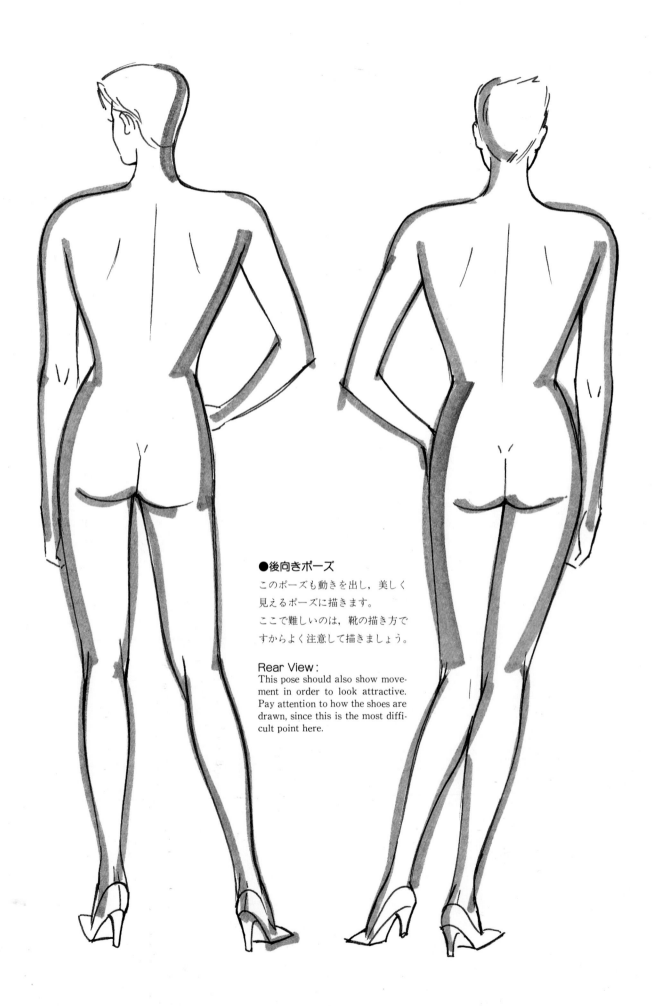

●後向きポーズ

このポーズも動きを出し，美しく
見えるポーズに描きます。
ここで難しいのは，靴の描き方で
すからよく注意して描きましょう。

Rear View：
This pose should also show movement in order to look attractive.
Pay attention to how the shoes are
drawn, since this is the most difficult point here.

身体の動きによって，コスチュームが身体にフィットする部分と，離れる部分が違ってきます。
また，デザインによってスリムのコスチュームとビッグのコスチュームによっても違ってきます。描く時に自分でポーズをとって研究しましょう。

Whether or not the clothes fit closely to the body depends on body movement, as well as the particular design (loose or closely fitting). Try posing in different ways yourself when drawing such illustrations.

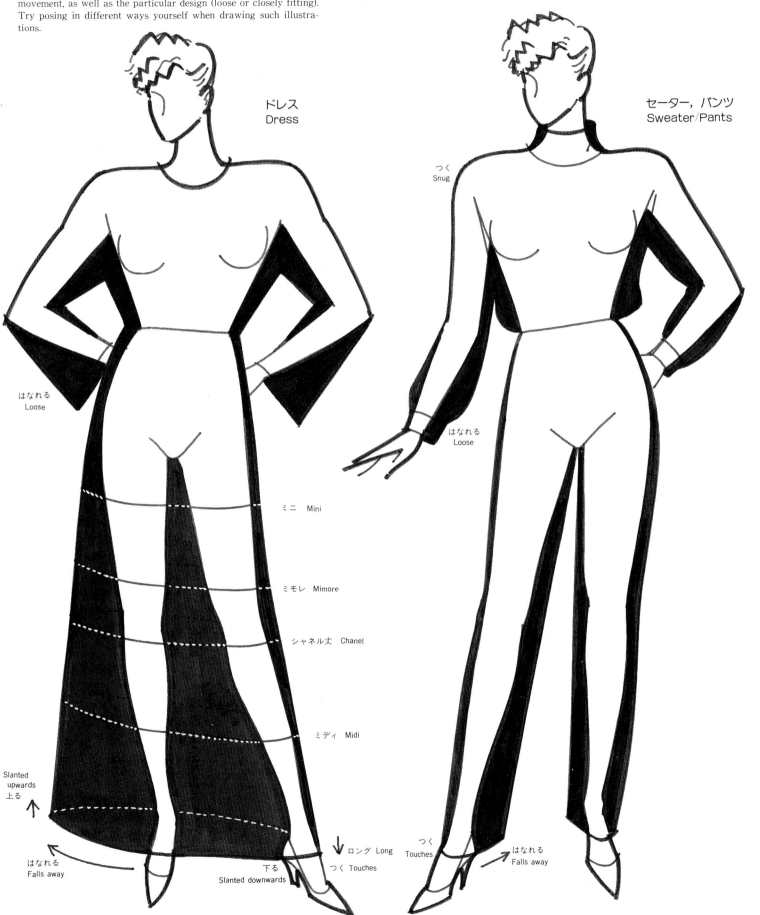

ドレス
Dress

セーター，パンツ
Sweater/Pants

つく
Snug

はなれる
Loose

はなれる
Loose

ミニ Mini

ミモレ Mimore

シャネル丈 Chanel

ミディ Midi

Slanted
upwards
上る

はなれる
Falls away

ロング Long
つく Touches
下る
Slanted downwards

つく
Touches

はなれる
Falls away

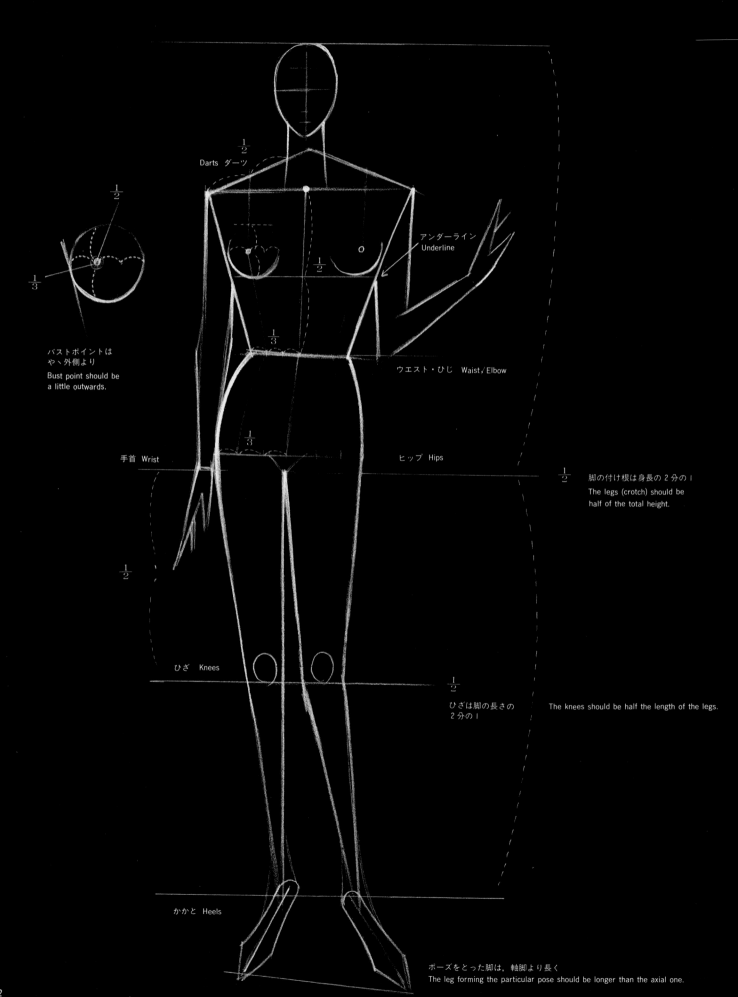

$\frac{1}{2}$

$\frac{1}{3}$

バストポイントは
や丶外側より
Bust point should be
a little outwards.

$\frac{1}{2}$

Darts ダーツ

アンダーライン
Underline

$\frac{1}{2}$

ウエスト・ひじ Waist／Elbow

$\frac{1}{3}$

手首 Wrist

$\frac{1}{3}$

ヒップ Hips

ポーズをとった脚は，軸脚より長く
The leg forming the particular pose should be longer than the axial one.

$\frac{1}{2}$

脚の付け根は身長の 2 分の I
The legs (crotch) should be
half of the total height.

$\frac{1}{2}$

ひざ Knees

$\frac{1}{2}$

ひざは脚の長さの
2 分の I

The knees should be half the length of the legs.

かかと Heels

ポーズをとった脚は，軸脚より長く
The leg forming the particular pose should be longer than the axial one.

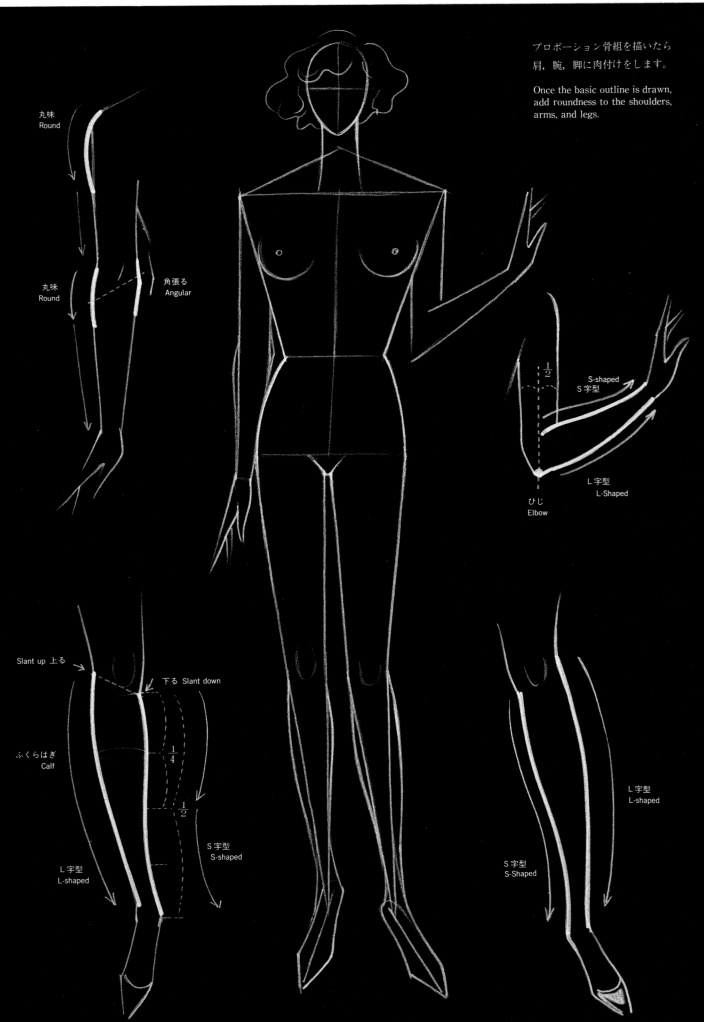

プロポーション骨組を描いたら
肩，腕，脚に肉付けをします。

Once the basic outline is drawn,
add roundness to the shoulders,
arms, and legs.

丸味
Round

丸味
Round

角張る
Angular

$\frac{1}{2}$

S-shaped
S 字型

L 字型
L-Shaped

ひじ
Elbow

Slant up 上る

下る Slant down

ふくらはぎ
Calf

$\frac{1}{4}$

$\frac{1}{2}$

S 字型
S-shaped

L 字型
L-shaped

L 字型
L-shaped

S 字型
S-Shaped

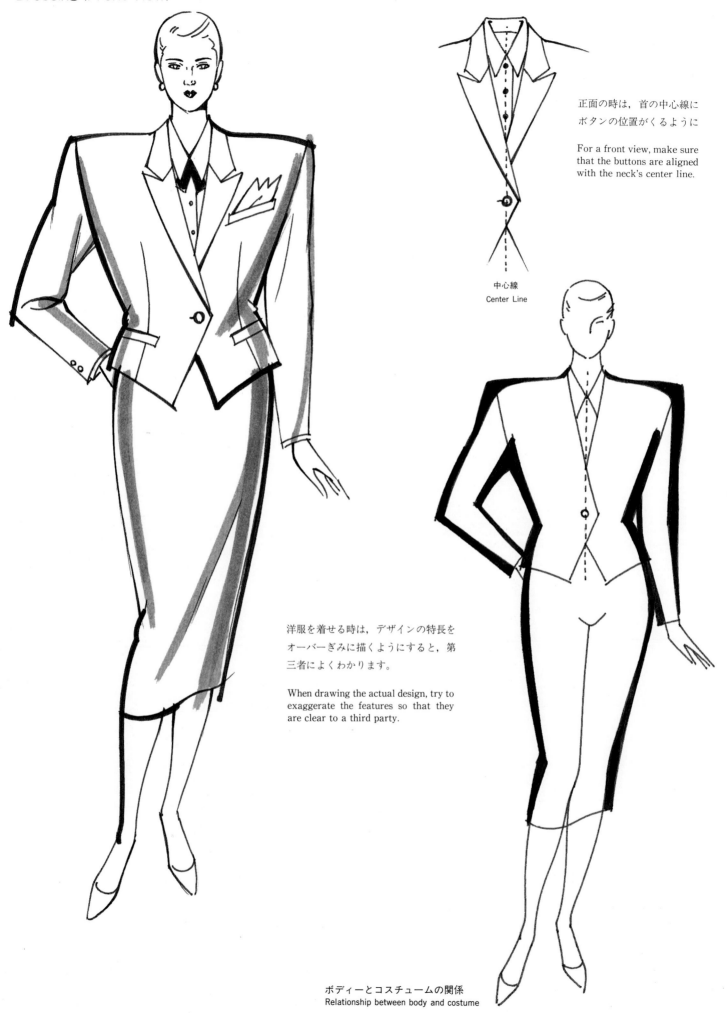

正面の時は，首の中心線に
ボタンの位置がくるように

For a front view, make sure
that the buttons are aligned
with the neck's center line.

中心線
Center Line

洋服を着せる時は，デザインの特長を
オーバーぎみに描くようにすると，第
三者によくわかります。

When drawing the actual design, try to
exaggerate the features so that they
are clear to a third party.

ボディーとコスチュームの関係
Relationship between body and costume

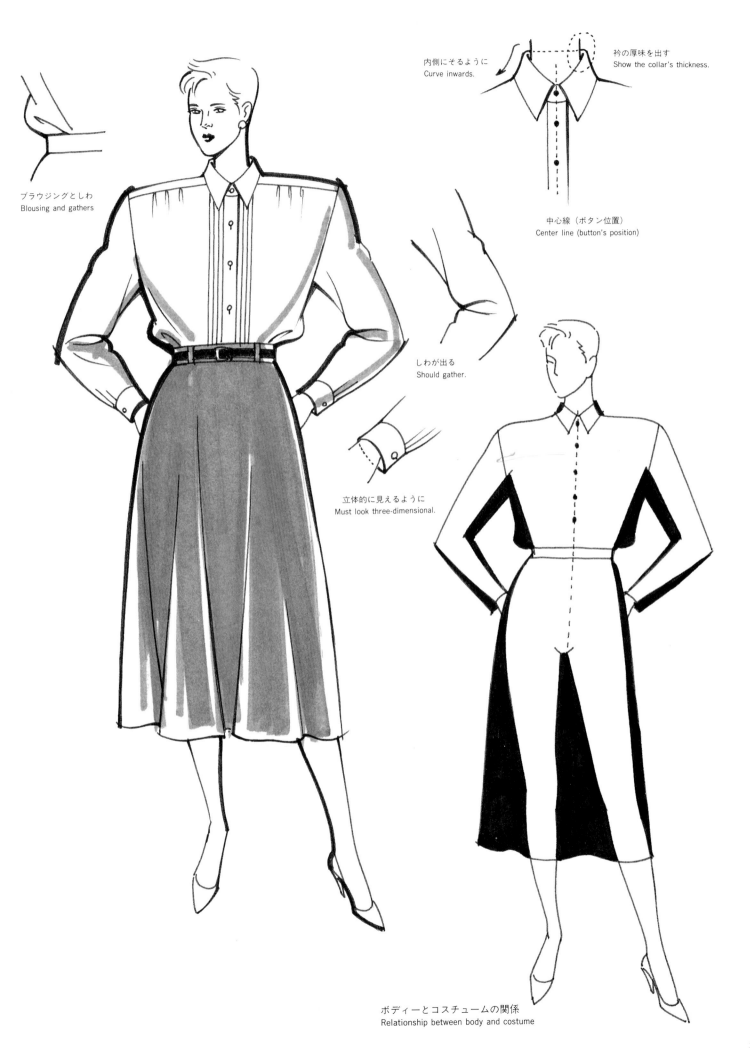

ブラウジングとしわ
Blousing and gathers

内側にそるように
Curve inwards.

衿の厚味を出す
Show the collar's thickness.

中心線（ボタン位置）
Center line (button's position)

しわが出る
Should gather.

立体的に見えるように
Must look three-dimensional.

ボディーとコスチュームの関係
Relationship between body and costume

着装（斜め向き）
Dressing (Oblique Profile)

サイドのデザインを説明する時には，斜めポーズを描きます。衿の大きさや，中心線が正面とは違ってきますので注意しましょう。

When explaining the design's side view, an oblique profile should be used. Pay attention to the collar's size and the center line, since they differ from a front view.

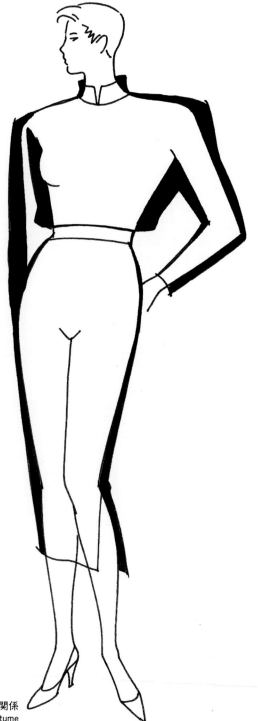

ボディーとコスチュームの関係
Relationship between body and costume

袖付けが内側に入る
Make sure that the armhole seam is inside.

パンツの時は，ひざのところにし
わが出ますので，よく研究しまし
ょう。

Study pants designs carefully,
remembering that the fabric tends
to gather around the knees.

ボディーとコスチュームの関係
Relationship between body and costume

着装（後向き）
Dressing (Back View)

後向きの時は，正面向きとはボディーのふくらみ方が違ってきますので，どこにしわが出るのか注意して下さい。

The body changes its fullness when viewed from behind.
Pay attention to which parts gather.

ボディーとコスチュームの関係
Relationship between body and costume

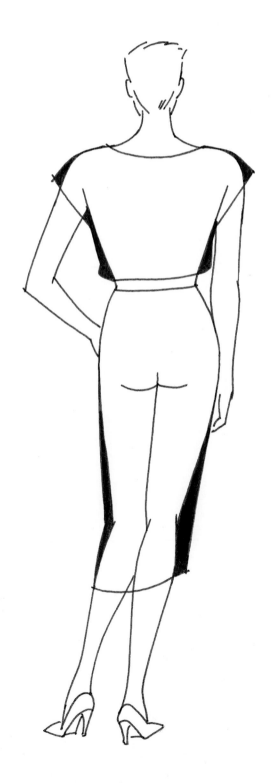

靴の描き方注意
Pay attention to how shoes are drawn.

輪郭線の強弱の付け方
Boldness of Lines

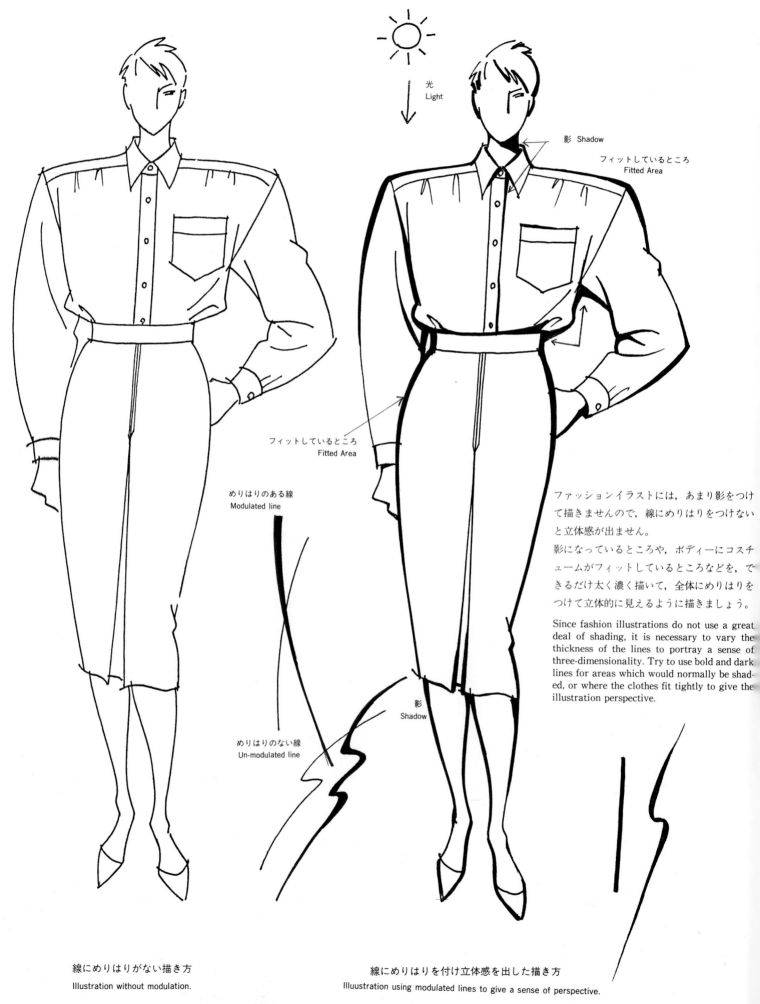

光
Light

影 Shadow

フィットしているところ
Fitted Area

フィットしているところ
Fitted Area

めりはりのある線
Modulated line

めりはりのない線
Un-modulated line

影
Shadow

ファッションイラストには，あまり影をつけて描きませんので，線にめりはりをつけないと立体感が出ません。

影になっているところや，ボディーにコスチュームがフィットしているところなどを，できるだけ太く濃く描いて，全体にめりはりをつけて立体的に見えるように描きましょう。

Since fashion illustrations do not use a great deal of shading, it is necessary to vary the thickness of the lines to portray a sense of three-dimensionality. Try to use bold and dark lines for areas which would normally be shaded, or where the clothes fit tightly to give the illustration perspective.

線にめりはりがない描き方
Illustration without modulation.

線にめりはりを付け立体感を出した描き方
Illustration using modulated lines to give a sense of perspective.

部分練習●衿の描き方
Practice of Individual Parts/Collar

正面向きボディー Front View of Body

斜め向きボディー Oblique Profile of Body

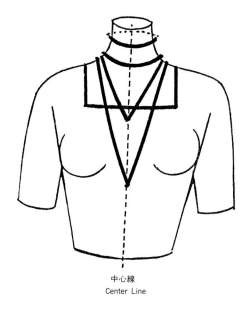

中心線
Center Line

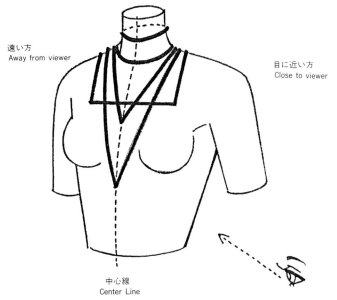

遠い方
Away from viewer

目に近い方
Close to viewer

中心線
Center Line

こゝから見たポーズ
Pose seen from this angle.

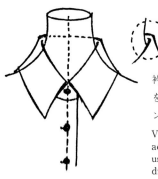

中心線（ボタンがくる）
Center Line (Buttons positioned here)

衿には生地の厚さによって，厚味をつけます。また衿はネックラインより少しはなすように。

Vary the thickness of the collar according to the type of fabric used. Also, the collar should be drawn slightly away from the neck.

中心線（ボタンがくる）
Center Line (Buttons positioned here)

中心線
Center Line

中心線
Center Line

重ね着をした時は，シャツと上着のボタンは，いつでも中心線の位置にきます。

When layering the clothes, remember that the buttons of both articles should be aligned with the center line.

袖とボトムのしわの描き方 Drawing Gathers (Wrinkles) on Sleeves and Pants

● 細みの袖のしわの出方 Gathers on Narrow Sleeves

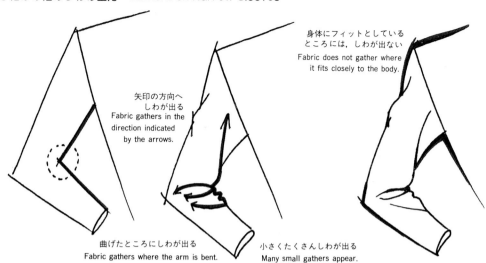

身体にフィットとしている
ところには，しわが出ない
Fabric does not gather where
it fits closely to the body.

矢印の方向へ
しわが出る
Fabric gathers in the
direction indicated
by the arrows.

曲げたところにしわが出る
Fabric gathers where the arm is bent.

小さくたくさんしわが出る
Many small gathers appear.

ファッションイラストでしわを描きわけることは大変重要です。しわを描くことによって，身体の動きや，ボディーの立体感，生地の質感を表現することができます。

ボディーの動きによって，しわの出方が違ってきます。

It is very important to be able to accurately portray gathers in fashion illustration. This gives the drawing perspective, portraying the body's movement and thickkness of fabric. The positioning of gathers depends on the body's movement.

● 太い袖のしわの出方 Gathers on Wide Sleeves

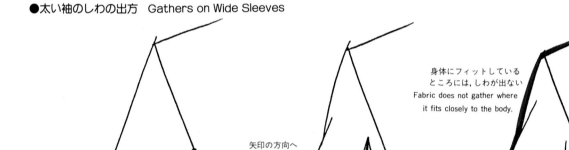

身体にフィットしている
ところには，しわが出ない
Fabric does not gather where
it fits closely to the body.

矢印の方向へ
しわが出る
Fabric gathers in the
direction indicated by
the arrows.

曲げたところにしわが出る
Fabric gathers where the arm is bent.

大きく少なめにしわが出る
A few large gathers appear.

● パンツのしわの出方 Gathers on Pants

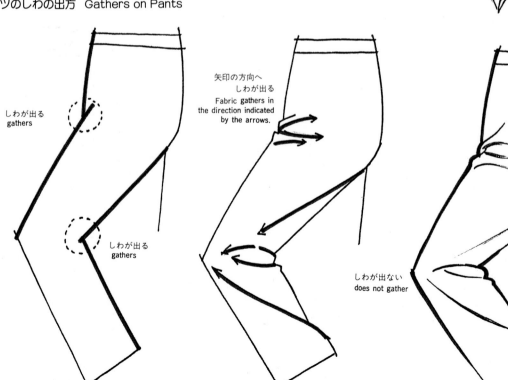

しわが出る
gathers

しわが出る
gathers

矢印の方向へ
しわが出る
Fabric gathers in
the direction indicated
by the arrows.

しわが出ない
does not gather

しわが出ない
does not gater

ギャザー＆フレアーの描き方
How to Draw Gathered and Flared Designs

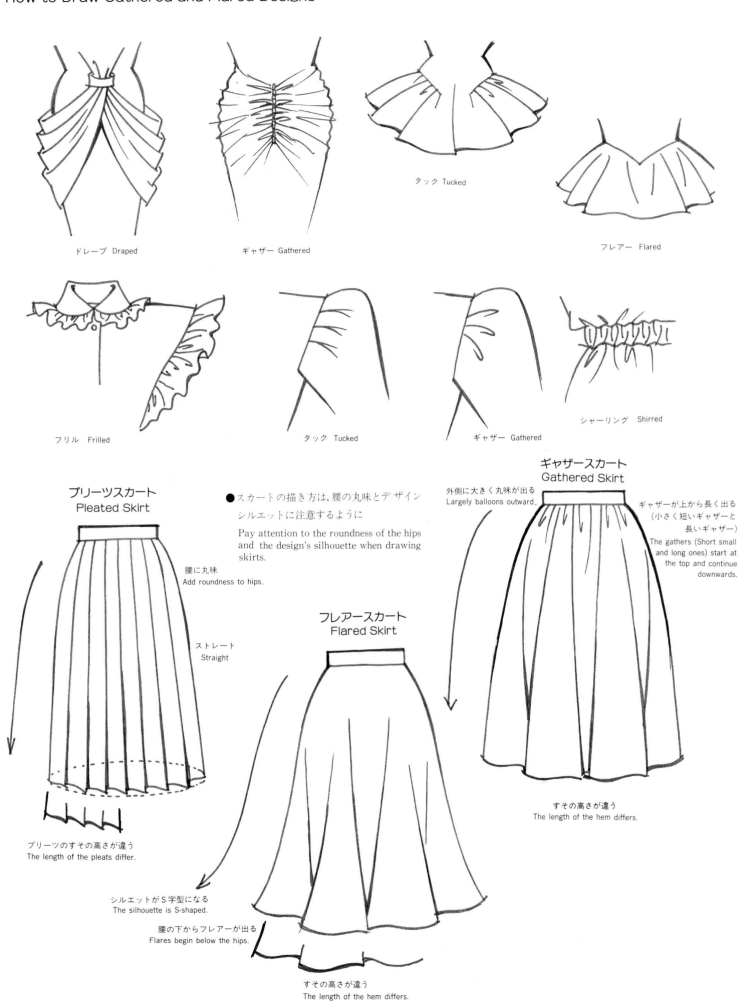

ドレープ Draped

ギャザー Gathered

タック Tucked

フレアー Flared

フリル Frilled

タック Tucked

ギャザー Gathered

シャーリング Shirred

プリーツスカート
Pleated Skirt

●スカートの描き方は，腰の丸味とデザインシルエットに注意するように

Pay attention to the roundness of the hips and the design's silhouette when drawing skirts.

腰に丸味
Add roundness to hips.

ストレート
Straight

プリーツのすその高さが違う
The length of the pleats differ.

シルエットがS字型になる
The silhouette is S-shaped.

腰の下からフレアーが出る
Flares begin below the hips.

フレアースカート
Flared Skirt

すその高さが違う
The length of the hem differs.

ギャザースカート
Gathered Skirt

外側に大きく丸味が出る
Largely balloons outward.

ギャザーが上から長く出る
（小さく短いギャザーと
長いギャザー）
The gathers (Short small and long ones) start at the top and continue downwards.

すその高さが違う
The length of the hem differs.

ディフォルメの描き方
How to Draw in Deformation

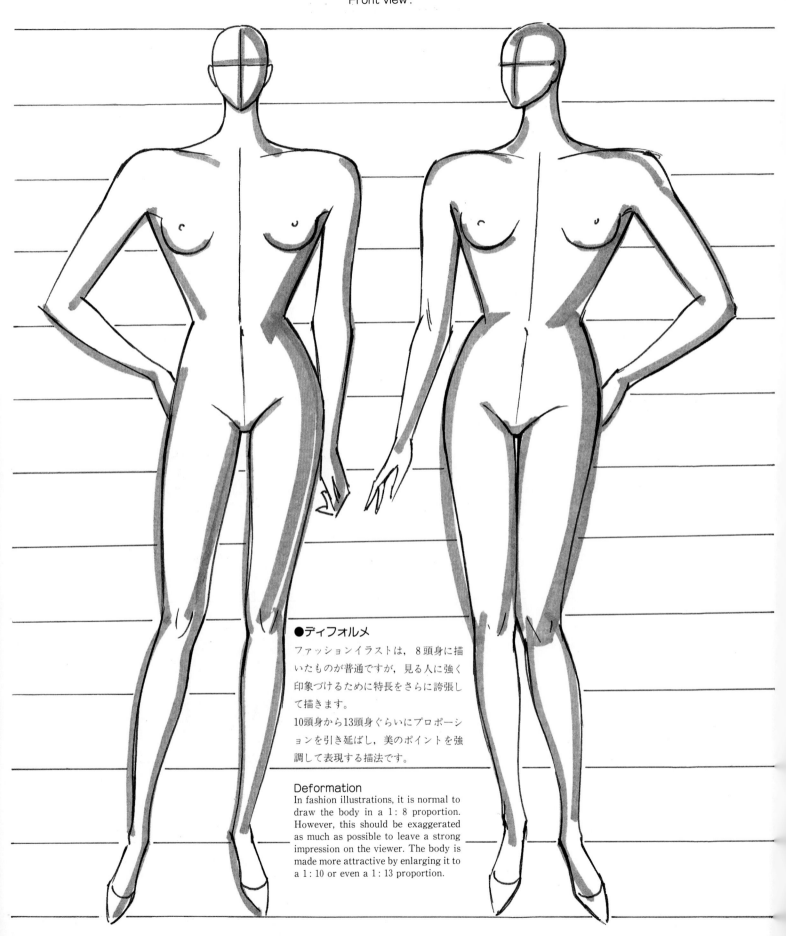

●ディフォルメ

ファッションイラストは，8頭身に描いたものが普通ですが，見る人に強く印象づけるために特長をさらに誇張して描きます。

10頭身から13頭身ぐらいにプロポーションを引き延ばし，美のポイントを強調して表現する描法です。

Deformation

In fashion illustrations, it is normal to draw the body in a 1 : 8 proportion. However, this should be exaggerated as much as possible to leave a strong impression on the viewer. The body is made more attractive by enlarging it to a 1 : 10 or even a 1 : 13 proportion.

正面向き着装
Front view (Dressed)

デザインの特長をできるだけ誇張して着装する
Dress the figure with the design's unique features exaggerated as much as possible.

ディフォルメの描き方
How to Draw in Deformation

斜め向きプロポーション
Oblique Profile

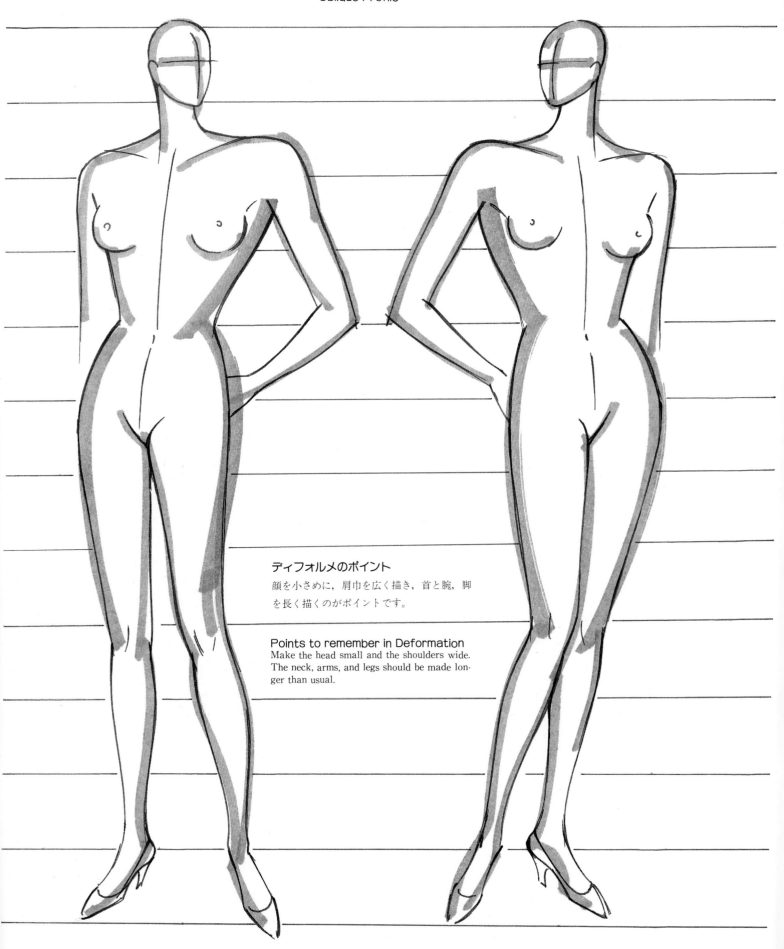

ディフォルメのポイント
顔を小さめに，肩巾を広く描き，首と腕，脚
を長く描くのがポイントです。

Points to remember in Deformation
Make the head small and the shoulders wide.
The neck, arms, and legs should be made lon-
ger than usual.

斜め向き着装
Oblique Profile (Dressed)

デザインシルエット●
Design Silhouettes

ウェステッド・ラインⅠ
Waisted Lines I

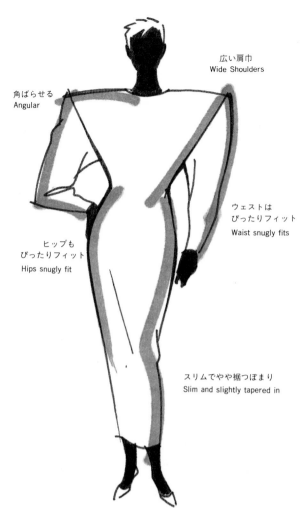

広い肩巾
Wide Shoulders

角ばらせる
Angular

ウェストは
ぴったりフィット
Waist snugly fits

ヒップも
ぴったりフィット
Hips snugly fit

スリムでやや裾つぼまり
Slim and slightly tapered in

プロのデザイナーの人達がデザインを考える時には，まず最初に全体のデザインシルエットを考えて描き始めると思います。

このデザインシルエットを知って，デザインを考える人と，そうでない人とでは，スピードも仕上り方も違ってきます。このシルエットの特長をできるだけ多く知っておくことが大切です。

Most professional designers first visualize the silhouette of the design. The completed illustration, and the speed in which it is completed, depends greatly on whether or not this silhouette is understood. It is important to know as many of the silhouette's unique features as possible.

●デザインシルエット参考例
Examples of Design Silhouette:

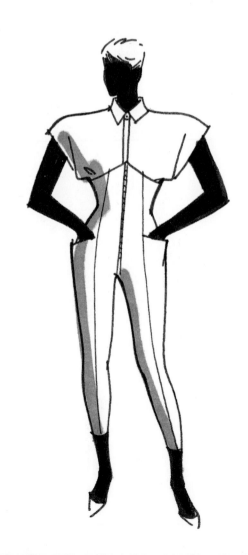

ウェステッド・ラインⅡ
Waisted Lines Ⅱ

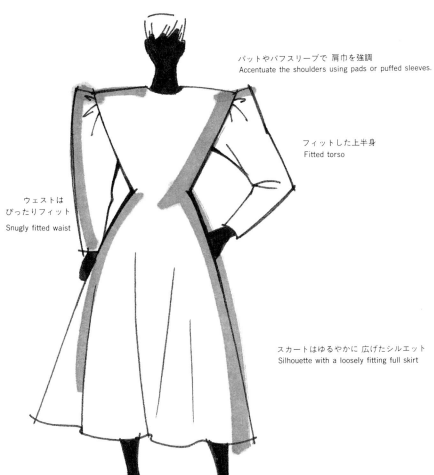

パットやパフスリーブで 肩巾を強調
Accentuate the shoulders using pads or puffed sleeves.

フィットした上半身
Fitted torso

ウェストは
ぴったりフィット
Snugly fitted waist

スカートはゆるやかに 広げたシルエット
Silhouette with a loosely fitting full skirt

● デザインシルエット参考例
Examples of Design Silhouettes :

トライアングル・ライン
Triangular Lines

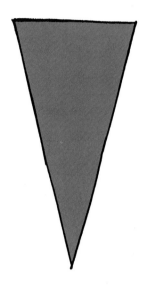

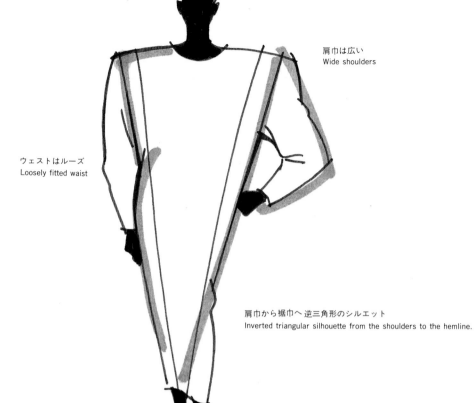

肩巾は広い
Wide shoulders

ウェストはルーズ
Loosely fitted waist

肩巾から裾巾へ逆三角形のシルエット
Inverted triangular silhouette from the shoulders to the hemline.

● デザインシルエット参考例
Examples of Design Silhouettes :

ストレート・ライン
Straight Lines

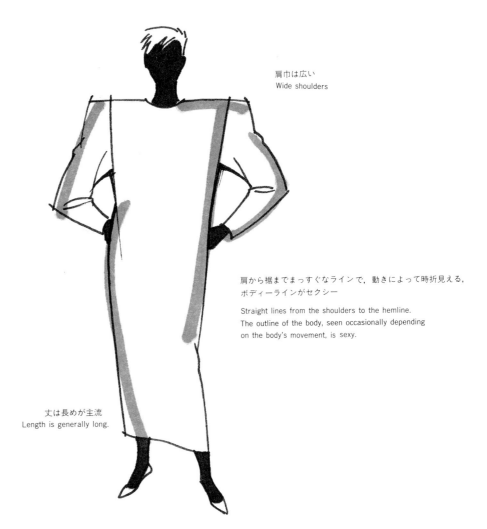

肩巾は広い
Wide shoulders

肩から裾までまっすぐなラインで，動きによって時折見える，ボディーラインがセクシー

Straight lines from the shoulders to the hemline.
The outline of the body, seen occasionally depending
on the body's movement, is sexy.

丈は長めが主流
Length is generally long.

●デザインシルエット参考例
Examples of Design Silhouettes:

アンプル・ライン
Ample Lines

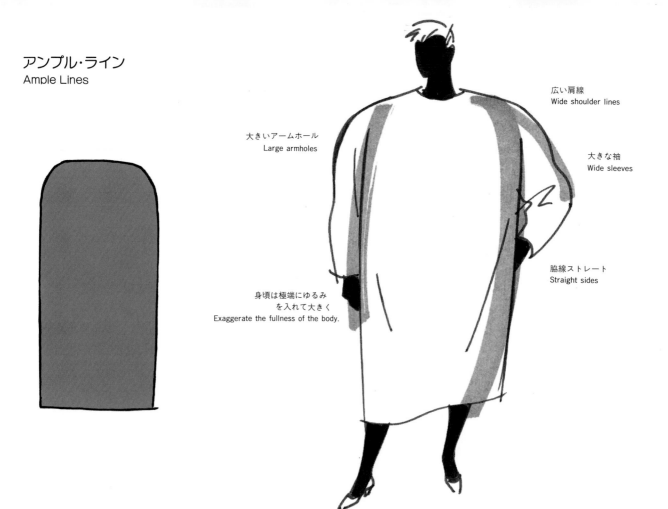

大きいアームホール
Large armholes

広い肩線
Wide shoulder lines

大きな袖
Wide sleeves

脇線ストレート
Straight sides

身頃は極端にゆるみ
を入れて大きく
Exaggerate the fullness of the body.

●デザインシルエット参考例
Examples of Design Silhouettes:

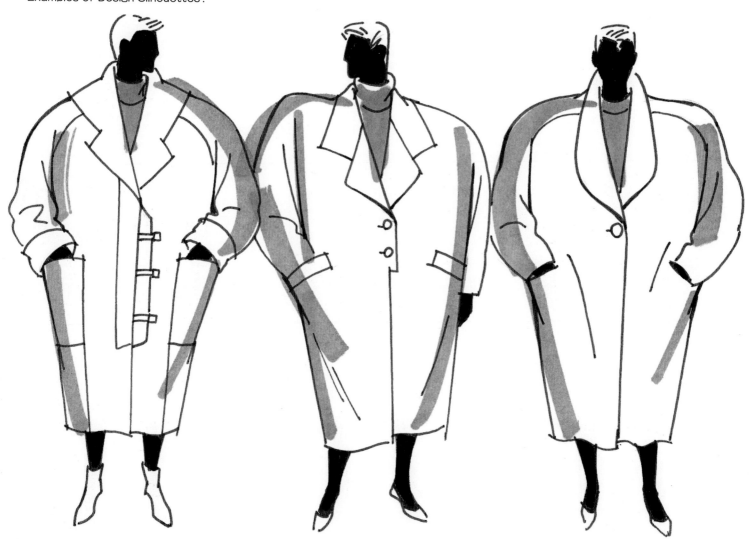

アワーグラス・ライン
Hourglass Lines

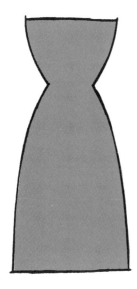

広い肩巾
Wide shoulders

たっぷり
ブラウジング
Plenty of blousing

ウエストは ぴったりフィット
Snugly fitted waist

ギャザーやプリーツで 腰回りにゆとりを
Give fullness to hips using gathers and pleats.

ふくらませたシルエット
Full silhouette

● デザインシルエット参考例
Examples of Design Silhouettes:

エッグ・ライン
Egglines

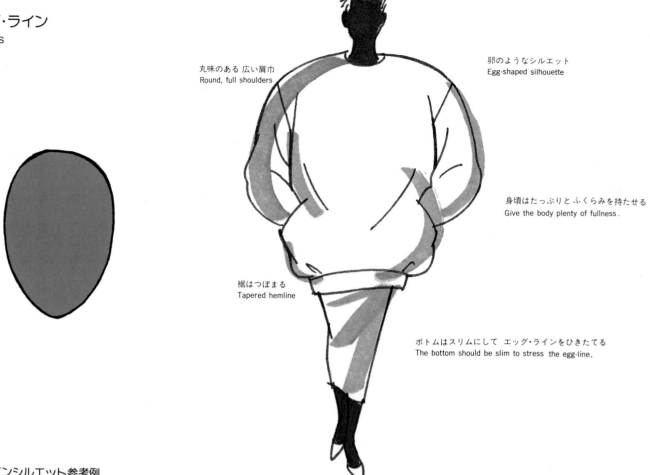

丸味のある 広い肩巾
Round, full shoulders

卵のようなシルエット
Egg-shaped silhouette

身頃はたっぷりと ふくらみを持たせる
Give the body plenty of fullness.

裾はつぼまる
Tapered hemline

ボトムはスリムにして エッグ・ラインをひきたてる
The bottom should be slim to stress the egg-line.

● デザインシルエット参考例
Examples of Design Silhouettes:

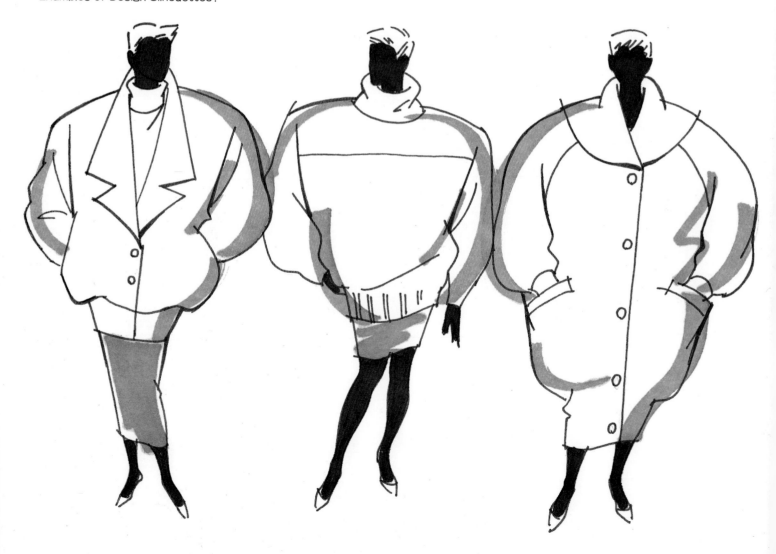

コスチューム・パターン画の描き方
How To Draw Costume Patterns :

ワンピース パターン画
Pattern for one-Piece Dress

Those who plan to become, as well as professional designers, must first learn to express their design (ideas) to a third party. It is therefore necessary to be able to effectively draw fashion illustrations. Even if the idea (design) is good, it is useless if this cannot be put down on paper.

Whithout drawing the body, first practice drawing the design (pattern) alone.

Once you learn to draw the costume (design), then all you need to do is draw is in the uncovered parts of the body (face, hands, and legs), This will complete the fashion illustration. Also, by leaving the body's movement alone and changing one element, such as the head's angle or the arms or legs, the illustration will be given a new atmosphere.

パターン画に顔や手，脚を描き込む
Add the face, hands, and legs to the pattern.

●応用
顔と腕のポーズを変える
Application：Change the angle of the face and arms.

上着パターン画
Jacket Pattern

ボトムパターン画 Bottom (Skirt) Pattern

顔，手，脚を描き込む
Add the face, hands, and legs.

●応用
顔，腕，脚のポーズを変える
Application : Change the angle of the face, arms, and legs.

上下を着た状態にする
Draw the pattern with the jacket and skirt.

47

ジャケット＆ボトム パターン画
Pattern for Jacket and Bottom (Pants)

ジャケットパターン画
Jacket Pattern

顔，手，脚を描き込む

Add the face, hands, and legs.

●応用

顔，腕，脚のポーズを変える

Application：Change the angle of the face, arms, and legs.

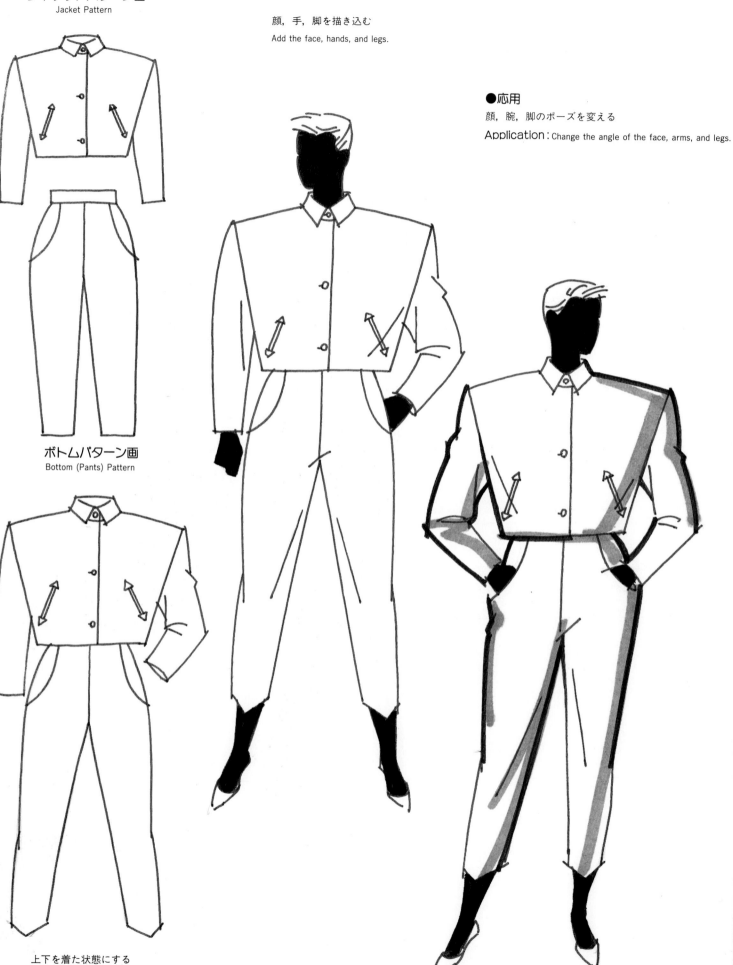

ボトムパターン画
Bottom (Pants) Pattern

上下を着た状態にする

Draw the Pattern with the jacket and pants.

How to draw the pattern
of the fabric :

How to add color :

柄の描き方 ● Adding Patterns to the Fabric

ストライプの描き方

ストライプの描き方で注意しなければならないのは，身頃と衿のストライプの流れが違っていることです。
身頃やボトムのストライプは，中心線にそって平行に描き入れ，スーツのような衿は，上衿と下衿のストライプが違ってきますので，注意して見ましょう。

How to Draw Stripes

When drawing stripes, remember that the direction of the stripes is different in the body and the collar. Stripes in the body and lower garment (skirt/pants) must be drawn parallel to the center line. Pay special attention to stripes in suit collars, since the upper one and lower one will differ.

ストライプ

柄の種類は無限ですが，まずポピュラーな柄の描き方をマスターしましょう。
ファッションイラストの場合には，あまり全体に柄を描き込まずに，ダーツやディテールのデザインがわかるように省略して描きましょう。

Stripes:
Although the variety of patterns is infinite, it is important to first master the basic ones.
For fashion illustrations, it is important to keep the fabric's pattern simple, concentrating on the darts and other details.

ヘリンボーンの幅をストライプのように，う
すく鉛筆で描き込みます。

Lightly draw the vertical lines with a pencil as you
would with stripes.

ストライプで描いたわくの中に，サインペン
でヘリンボーンの柄を描き入れます。

Use a felt-tip pen to draw in the herringbone pattern
within the stripes.

千鳥格子の描き方
How to Draw Hound's-tooth Patterns

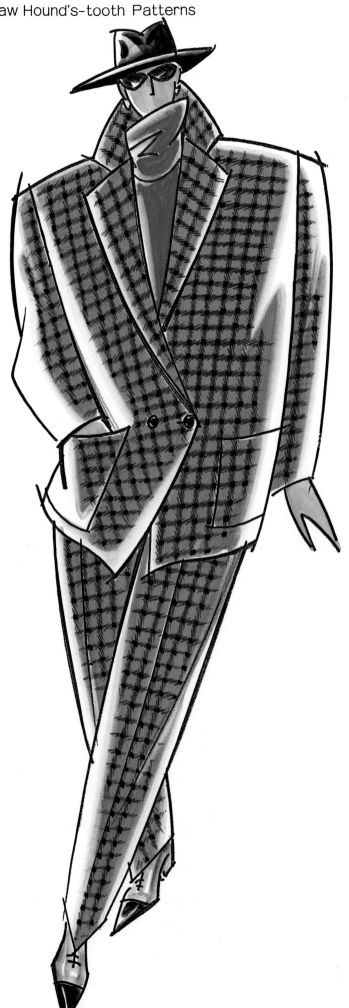

コスチューム全体に鉛筆で格子にうすく描き込みます。

Using a pencil, lightly draw in the checkered pattern on the entire costume.

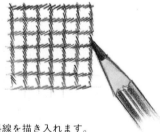

濃い鉛筆で斜線を描き入れます。

Use a dark pencil to draw in oblique lines.

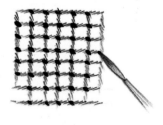

格子の交っているところに，小筆でポスターカラーの黒を塗っていきます。

Use a small brush to color in the areas where the lines cross with black poster color.

最初，コスチューム全体に地の色を塗ります。
First color in the base color (entire costume).

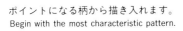

ポイントになる柄から描き入れます。
Begin with the most characteristic pattern.

色の組合せを考えて，次の色を入れます。
With the combination of attractive colors in mind, apply the next color.

最後に明るい色を入れます。
Use the lightest color last.

クレヨンとローソクを使った描き方
How to Draw Patterns Using Crayons and Wax

ニットなどの柄や編地を，クレヨンやローソクなどを使って描くと，ニットのソフトな風合を出すことができます。

For drawing patterns on knits, or when portraying the knit fabric itself, crayons or wax should be used to show the softness of the fabric.

ローソク
Wax

クレヨン
Crayon

クレヨンやローソクで描き入れます。
Use a crayon or wax to draw the pattern.

描き込んだ上から水彩絵具で，地の色を塗っていきます。

Use water colors to paint over the pattern with the base color.

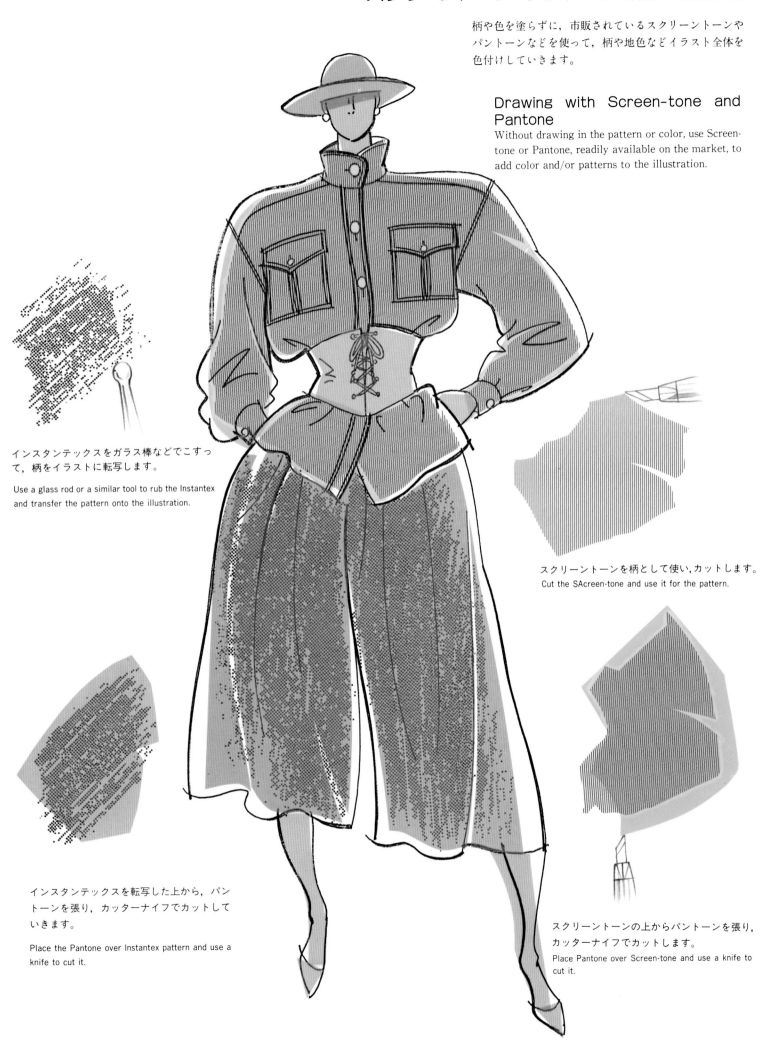

柄や色を塗らずに，市販されているスクリーントーンやパントーンなどを使って，柄や地色などイラスト全体を色付けしていきます。

Drawing with Screen-tone and Pantone

Without drawing in the pattern or color, use Screen-tone or Pantone, readily available on the market, to add color and/or patterns to the illustration.

インスタンテックスをガラス棒などでこすって，柄をイラストに転写します。

Use a glass rod or a similar tool to rub the Instantex and transfer the pattern onto the illustration.

スクリーントーンを柄として使い，カットします。

Cut the SAcreen-tone and use it for the pattern.

インスタンテックスを転写した上から，パントーンを張り，カッターナイフでカットしていきます。

Place the Pantone over Instantex pattern and use a knife to cut it.

スクリーントーンの上からパントーンを張り，カッターナイフでカットします。

Place Pantone over Screen-tone and use a knife to cut it.

色の塗り方 ● Adding Color

水 彩
Water Colors

①全体に大筆に色を多量に含ませ，うすめに
省略的に塗ります。

Absorb the paint in a large brush and use it to
color in the illustration. Only a thin coat of paint
should be applied here.

②その上に重ね塗りし，イラストの外側にぼ
かしていきます。

Apply a second coat in the same way, adding
gradation towards the edges.

④広いところが塗り終ったら，細かいところのコスチュームや肌色，メークなどを塗り仕上りです。

Complete the illustration by coloring in the details, such as the skin and make-up.

③全体に，しわと影を描き込みめりはりをつけます。

Modulate the illustration by adding gathers, wrinkles, and shadows.

ポスターカラー
Poster Colors

①上下をベタ塗りで省略的に塗ります。

Roughly paint both the top and bottom garments.

②筆に水を含ませ，外側にグラデーションにぼかしていきます。

Absorb water into the brush and add gradation towards the edges.

④顔や腕，脚に肌の色を付け，ヘアの色やメークを入れ
　て仕上りです。

Complete the illustration by adding color to the face, arms,
legs, hair, and make-up.

③身頃に色むらができたら，もう一度身頃の中央をベタ
　塗りします。

If the color is uneven on the body, once more.

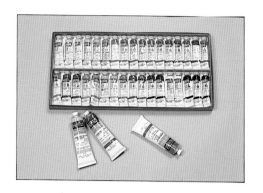

リキテックス
Liquitex

①といたリキテックスの色を，最初はうすく
大まかに塗ります。

Roughly apply a thin coat of dissolved Liquitex.

②さらに色が乾いたら，最初の色よりうすく
上から重ね塗りします。

When the first coat is dry, apply an even thinner
one over it.

③2～3回うすく重ね塗りしたら，最後に濃い色で塗り，
乾かないうちに筆の色を水で洗ってから，グラデーシ
ョンにぼかします。

After applying two or three thin coats, apply a heavier one,
using a dark color. Before the Liquitex dries, wet the brush
and add gradation to the illustration.

④最後にしわや影を入れ，めりはりをつけます。
肌色とヘア・メークを描き入れ仕上げです。

Add gathers, wrinkles, and shadows to modulate
the illustration. complete the drawing by coloring in
the skin, hair and make-up.

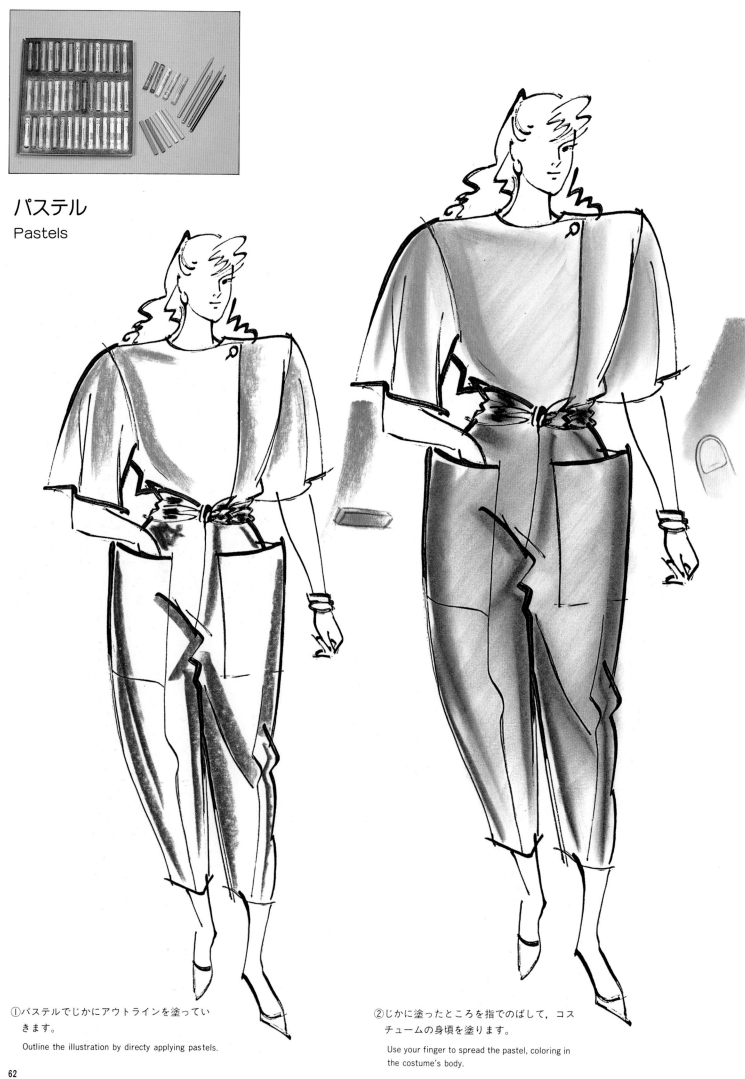

パステル
Pastels

①パステルでじかにアウトラインを塗っていきます。

Outline the illustration by directy applying pastels.

②じかに塗ったところを指でのばして, コスチュームの身頃を塗ります。

Use your finger to spread the pastel, coloring in the costume's body.

③コスチュームのしわや明るいところに，練りゴムや
消しゴムなどを使って，明るく描き入れます。

Use a paste or regular eraser to apply wrinkles, gathers, and
light areas.

④肌色やヘア・メークなどを描き，バックにパステルで
タッチを付けたりしながら，イラストに動きなどを出
します。

Give the illustration movement by coloring in the skin and
hair, adding make-up, and by touching up the background
with pastels.

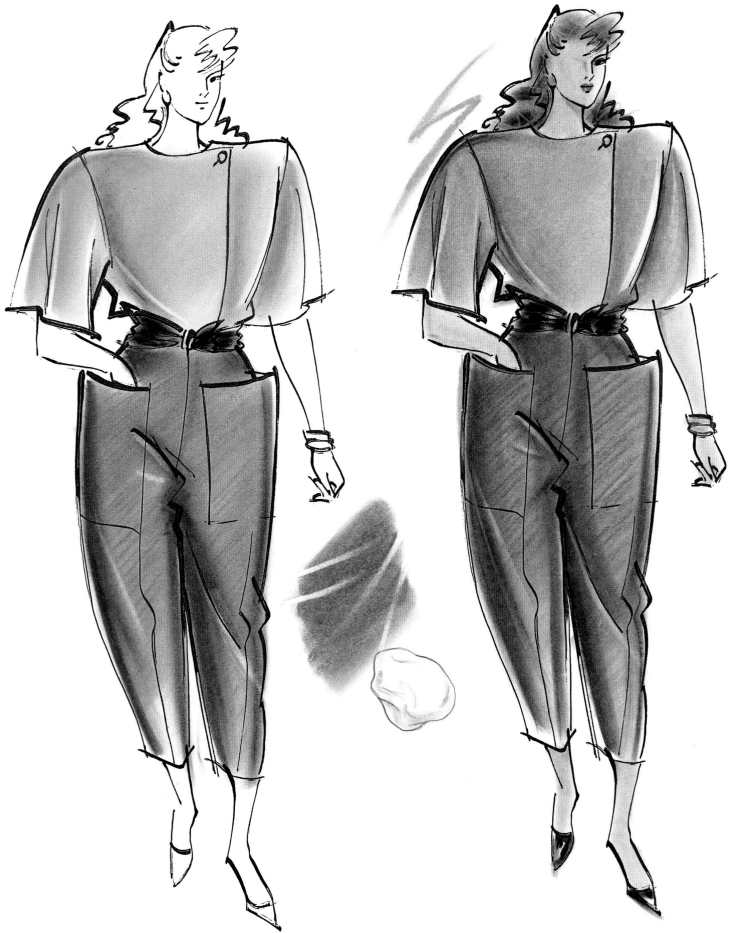

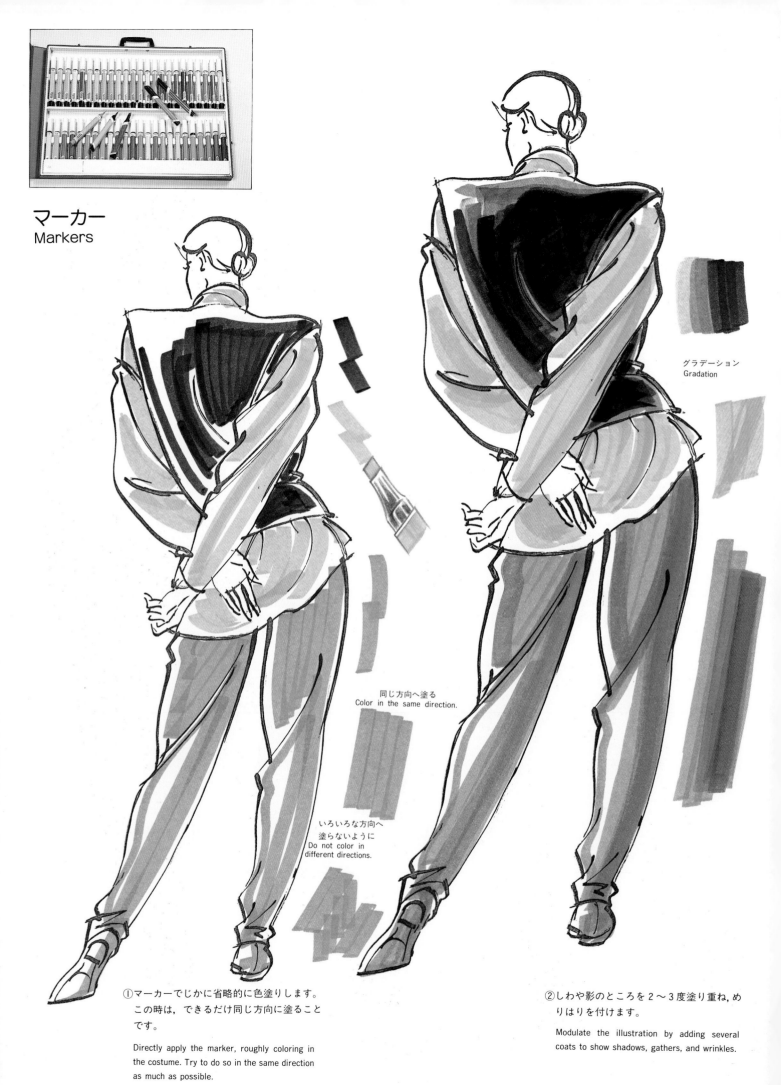

マーカー
Markers

グラデーション
Gradation

同じ方向へ塗る
Color in the same direction.

いろいろな方向へ
塗らないように
Do not color in
different directions.

①マーカーでじかに省略的に色塗りします。
この時は，できるだけ同じ方向に塗ること
です。

Directly apply the marker, roughly coloring in
the costume. Try to do so in the same direction
as much as possible.

②しわや影のところを2～3度塗り重ね，め
りはりを付けます。

Modulate the illustration by adding several
coats to show shadows, gathers, and wrinkles.

③しわや影を入れる時は，同系色かその色に
あうやっ濃い色を塗ります。

When shading or adding wrinkles and gathers,
use a similar shade to apply a slightly darker
color to these areas.

影になるところをもっと濃くする
時は，同系色の濃い色で塗る
To make the shaded areas darker,
apply a similar, but darker color.

④ヘアや肌色を入れ仕上りです。

Complete the illustration by adding color to the
skin and hair.

ファッションイラストレーションを描く際，布地の持つ
材質感をどのように表現するかが，描き手にとって重要
な要素です。

まず洋服を描く前にどのように見えるか，どのように感
じるかを考えます。例えば，柔らかさ，粗さ，なめらか
さ，光沢，透明感，張り具合などです。

ギャザーやフリル，ヘムライン，袖口は布地により，そ
してさまざまな量感によって変化します。

いろいろと質感の違うものを手にし，実際に着ている物
を見て，しわの出方や肌ざわりの違いを研究しましょう。

Drawing Different Fabrics :
Perhaps the most important aspect of an illustration is
how accurately the fabric's texture and unique qualities
are expressed.
Before beginning the illustration it is first necessary to
think about how the fabric appears and feels. This includes
aspects such as the fabric's softness, roughness, smooth-
ness, luster, and transparency. Gathers, frills, the hem-line,
and sleeves will all vary according to the fabric. In order
to study the difference in texture and how each fabric
falls, try to feel as many different types of fabrics as
possible, and look at actual clothes made of them.

素材の描き方

ニット／ラメ／デニム
ベルベット／キルティング
ツイード＆ヘリンボーン
ビニール／バックスキン
ムートン／光沢のあるレザー
レオパード／ミンク

How to Draw Fabric

Knits / Lamé / Denim /
Velvet / Quilting /
Tweed and Herringbone /
Viny / Coatings / Buckskin /
Sheepskin / Shiny Leather /
Leopard-skin / Mink

素材の描き方 ● How to Draw Fabric

ニットの描き方 How to Draw Knits

画材・パステル
用紙・画用紙

Method： Pastels
Peper： Drawing Paper

①パステルをじかに，コスチュームのアウト
　ラインに塗ります。

Directly apply the pastel to the costume's outline.

仕上り
Completed View

じかに塗る
Directly apply

①

②指でのばして塗ります。
Spread the color with your finger.

③ ①②と同じように塗ります。
Repeat steps 1) and 2).

指でのばして塗る
Use your finger to spread
the color.

①②と同じ
Same as 1) and 2).

②

③

④色鉛筆で編地を入れます。
Use a colored pencil to add the knitted pattern.

⑤肌色やヘア・メークを入れて仕上りです。
Complete the illustration by adding color to the
skin, hair, and make-up.

編地を入れる
Add the knitted pattern.

④

⑤

ラメの描き方　How to Draw Lamé

画材・パステル，ポスターカラー
用紙・ケント紙

Method : Pastels, Poster Colors
Paper : Kent Paper

①デザイン，ディテールを残しながら，パステルで省略的に塗ります。

Roughtly color in the costume with pastels, leaving out the details.

仕上り
Completed View

①

②じかに塗りたいところを指でぼかしていきます。
Add gradation by using your finger to rub and spread the color.

③光っているところやギャザーなどのところを，練りゴムで明るく描き入れます。
Use a paste eraser to show gathers and shiny areas.

指でこする
Rub with finger.

練りゴムで明るいところを描き入れる
Use a paste eraser to show the shiny areas.

②

③

④ラメが光っているところは，ポスターカラーのホワイトを筆で描き入れます。

Use a brush to draw in the lamé with a white poster color.

⑤肌色，ヘア・メーク，靴を塗り仕上りです。

Complete the illustration by coloring in the skin, hair, make-up, and shoes.

ホワイトで
ラメを入れる

Apply lamé with white.

④

⑤

デニムの描き方 How to Draw Denim

画材・水彩
用紙・画用紙

Method : Water Colors
Paper : Drawing Paper

①水彩で平面的に塗ります。
Evenly apply the paint (water color).

仕上り
Completed View

平面的に塗る
Evenly apply

①

②筆に水を付けこするようにして，画用紙の目が見えるように色むらをつくります。

Wet the brush with water and rub it into the paper until the texture can be seen and the color becomes uneven.

③しわと影を少し濃い色で描き込みます。セーターを塗ります。

Draw the shadows and wrinkles with a slightly darker shade. Color in the sweater.

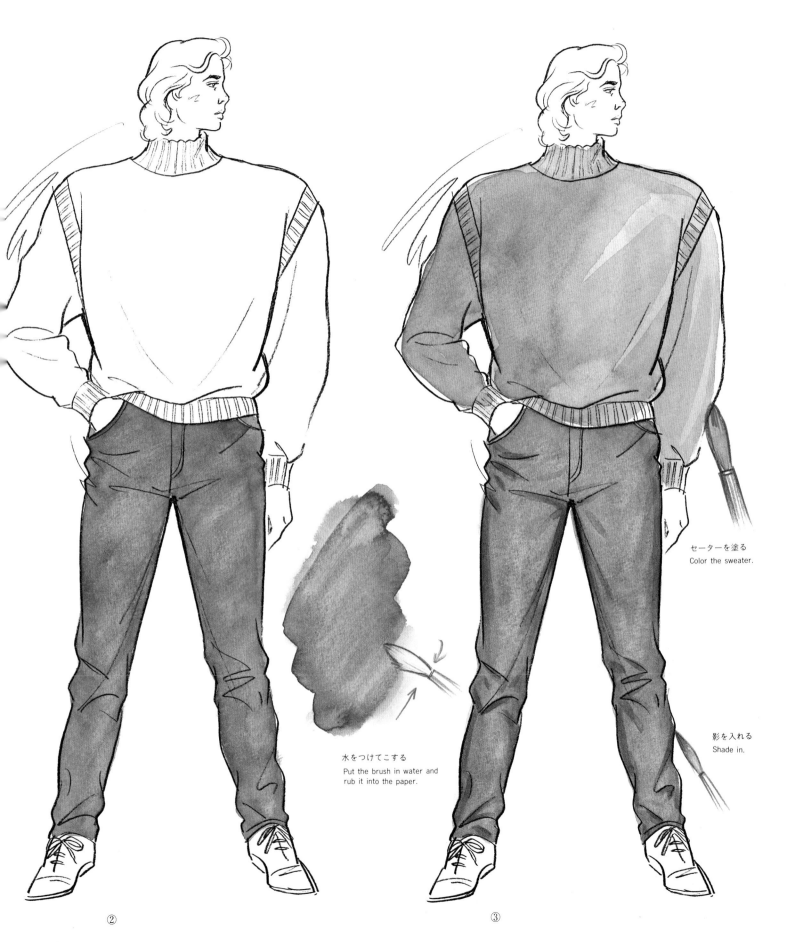

水をつけてこする
Put the brush in water and rub it into the paper.

セーターを塗る
Color the sweater.

影を入れる
Shade in.

②

③

④デニムにステッチを入れ，肌色と靴，ヘアなどに色を
付けます。

Draw in the stitches, and color the skin, hair, and shoes.

⑤靴やヘア，顔にめりはりをつけ，バックに色でタッチ
を入れて，ジーンズのラフな感じの効果をだします。

Modulate the shoes, hair, and face. Add color to the background to express the roughness of the jeans.

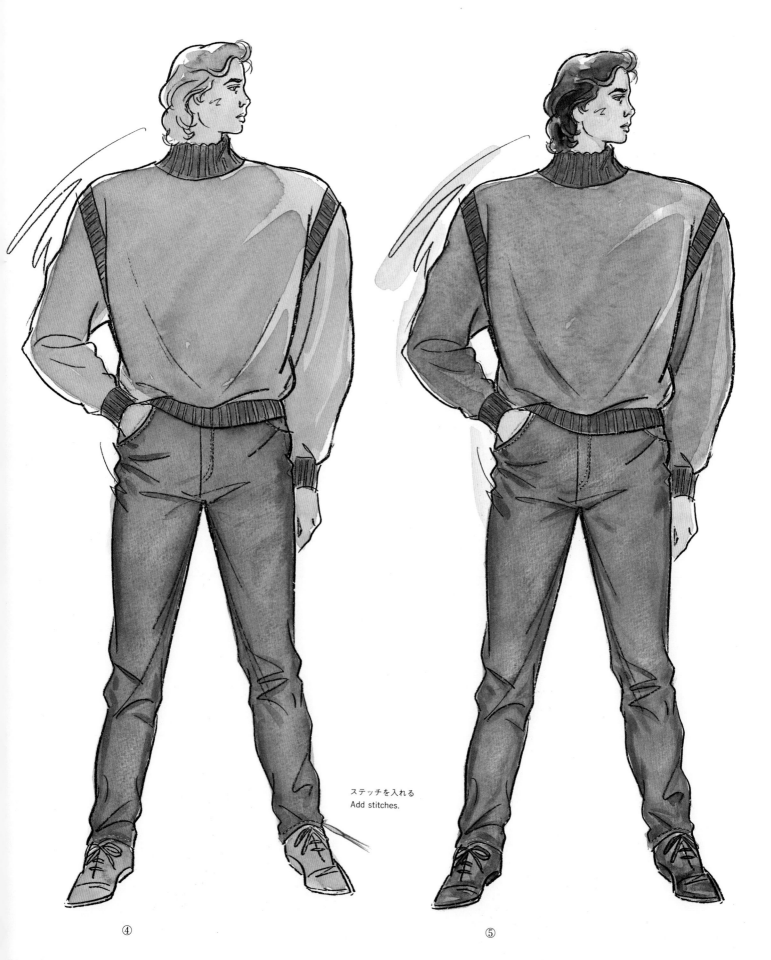

ステッチを入れる
Add stitches.

④

⑤

ベルベットの描き方 How to Draw Velvet

画材・ポスターカラー，色鉛筆
用紙・画用紙

Method : Poster Colors, Colored Pencils
Paper : Drawing Paper

①大きい筆でコスチュームを，うすめに平面的にベタ
塗りをします。

Use a large brush to evenly paint the costume with a light
shade.

仕上り
Completed View

大筆でベタ塗り
Use a large brush to
paint the costume.

①

77

②コスチューム全体にしわと影を入れます。
Add wrinkles, gathers, and shadows to the entire costume.

③ブラウスにも①②と同じように色を入れます。
Follow steps 1) and 2) to color the blouse.

影としわを入れる
Add shadows and wrinkles.

②

ブラウスに色をつける
Color the blouse.

③

④色鉛筆のホワイトで，しわと明るいところを描き入れます。

Add wrinkles and the light areas with a white colored pencil.

⑤肌色，ヘア・メーク，靴，アクセサリーを描き入れ，仕上りです。

Complete the illustration by coloring in the skin, hair, make-up, shoes, and accessories.

ホワイトで明るいところを描き入れる

Use a white pencil to add the light areas.

④

⑤

キルティングの描き方 How to Draw Quilting

画材・ポスターカラー
用紙・ケント紙

Method : Poster Colors
Paper : Kent Paper

①平面的にベタ塗りをします。
Evenly apply the color.

仕上り
Completed View

ベタ塗り
Color all over.

①

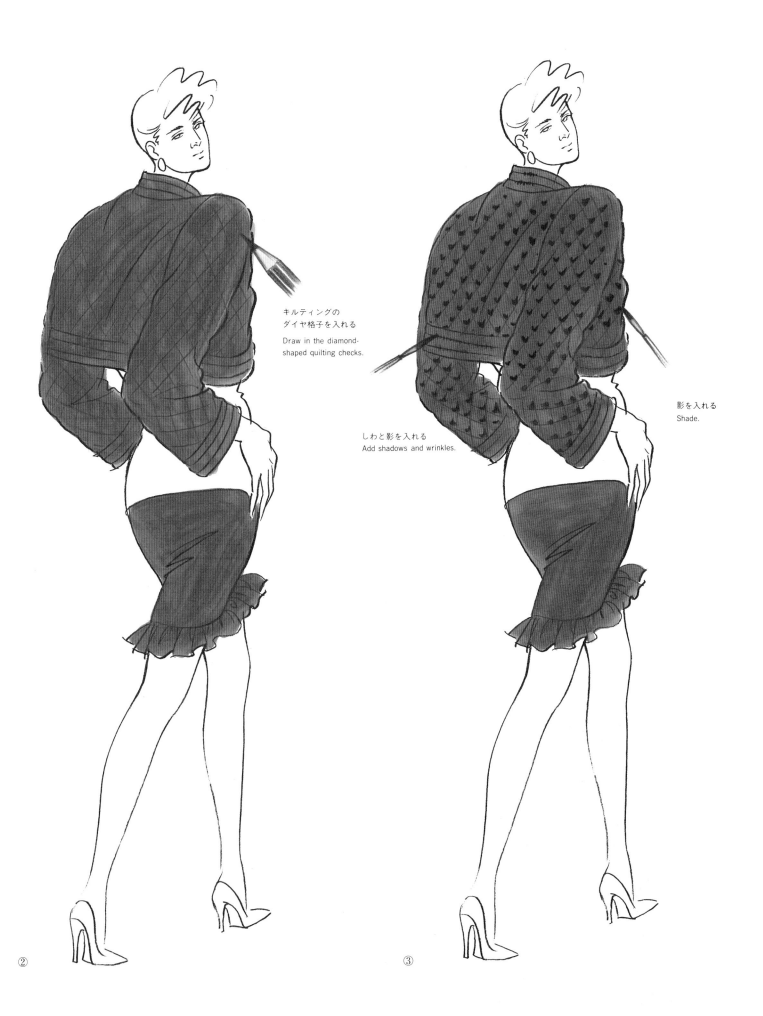

キルティングの
ダイヤ格子を入れる
Draw in the diamond-
shaped quilting checks.

しわと影を入れる
Add shadows and wrinkles.

影を入れる
Shade.

② 鉛筆でキルティングの幅にダイヤ格子を描きます。

Use a pencil to draw in diamond-shaped checks in the width of the quilting.

③ ダイヤ格子の中に，小筆で影を入れます。

Use a small brush to shade in the checks.

④全体に明るく光っているところにホワイトを入れ, し
　わや影に鉛筆でめりはりをつけます。

Use white to portray the light areas, and a pencil to modulate
the shadows and wrinkles.

⑤シャツやストッキング, 肌色, ヘア・メークを入れ仕
　上りです。

Complete the illustration by coloring in the shirt, stockings,
skin, hair, and make-up.

しわや影を入れる
Add shadows and wrinkles.

ホワイトで 光を入れる
Use white to show light areas.

④

⑤

ツイード＆ヘリンボーンの描き方
How to Draw Tweed and Herringbone Patterns

画材・ポスターカラー
用紙・ケント紙

Method: Poster Colors
Paper: Kent Paper

①ポスターカラーでコスチュームの外側を多めに残し、ベタ塗りします。

Apply poster color to the costume, leaving the edges uncolored.

仕上り
Completed View

①

ベタ塗り
Color all over.

ベタ塗り
Color all over.

③しわと影を入れ，スーツのヘリンボーンを鉛筆で描き込みます。

Add shadows and wrinkles, and then use a pencil to draw in the herringbone pattern of the suit.

ヘリンボーンを描
Draw the herringbone patte

ぼかす
Smudge to add gradation.

しわと影を入れる
Add shadows
and wrinkles.

②

②筆に水を少しつけて，ベタ塗りしたところのふちを，グラデーションにぼかしていきます。

Add gradation to the edges by placing the brush in a little water.

③

⑤マフラー，靴，肌，ヘアを色付けして仕上げます。
Color the scarf, shoes, skin, and hair to complete the illustration.

筆先をバサバサにする
Keep the brush semi-dry.

④筆の先にあまり水をつけないで，バサバサにして，ツイードの感じに全体を色付けしていきます。

Without adding too much water to the brush, apply color to show the tweed fabric (the brush should be quite dry).

④

⑤

①マーカーで省略的にじか塗りします。
Directly apply the marker to partially color
the costume.

画材・マーカー
用紙・ケント紙

Method： Markers
Paper： Kent Paper

じか塗り
Directly apply.

仕上り
Completed View

①

②ベタ塗りしたふちを，透明なマーカーを使いぼかします。

Add gradation by using a transparent marker around the edges.

③色鉛筆のホワイトで光っているところを描き，一番明るく光っているところは，ポスターカラーのホワイトを入れます。

Use a white colored pencil to show the bright and shiny spots. Use a white poster color to show the brightest spots.

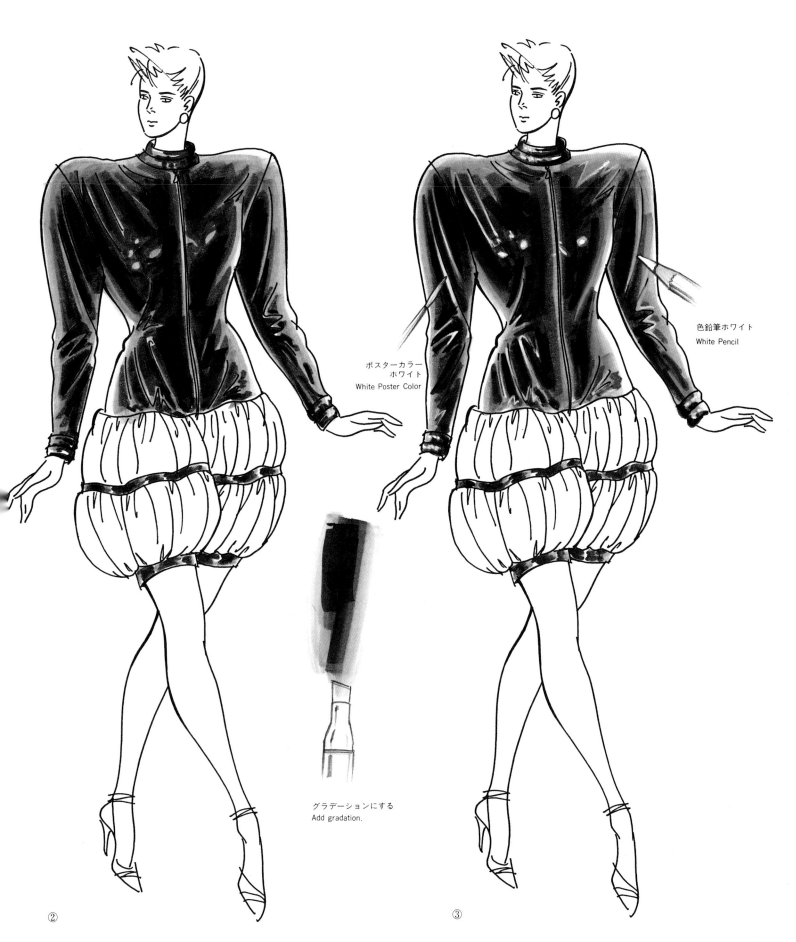

ポスターカラー
ホワイト
White Poster Color

色鉛筆ホワイト
White Pencil

グラデーションにする
Add gradation.

②

③

④ボトムやストッキングをグレーのマーカーで塗ります。

Use a gray marker for the lower garment and stockings.

⑤肌色，ヘア・メークを描き込み仕上りです。

Color the skin, hair, and make-up to complete the illustration.

しわ，影を入れる
Add shadows and wrinkles.

④

⑤

バックスキンの描き方 How to Draw Buckskin

画材・パステル，水彩

用紙・ケント紙

Methot：Pastels, Water Colors

Paper：Kent Paper

①パステルを別紙に塗りつけ，擦筆にその色をつけ，バックスキン上下に塗ります。

Apply the pastel to another piece of paper, and then onto a stump. Use the stump to apply the color to the top and bottom of the costume.

仕上り

Completed View

擦筆に色をつける

Apply the color to a stump.

擦筆で色を塗る

Use a stump to color in the costume.

①

89

②地色よりも濃い色を指につけ，むらをだしながら，こ
するようにして塗ります。

Apply a darker shade of pastel to your finger and unevenly rub
it in.

③練りゴムを使って明るいところを描き入れ，裏地や細
部は，パステル鉛筆で描いていきます。

Use a paste eraser to show the light areas. For the lining and
other small areas, use a pastel pencil.

濃い色を指で塗る
Apply a dark shade
with your finger.

パステル鉛筆
Pastel pencil

明るいところを
練りゴムで描く
Draw light areas with
a paste eraser.

②

③

④シャツや靴の色を水彩で塗ります。
Color the shirt and shoes with water colors.

⑤肌色，ヘア・メークの色付けをし仕上りです。
Color the skin, hair, and make-up to complete the illustration.

水彩で色付け
Use water colors.

④

⑤

ムートンの描き方 How to Draw Sheepskin

画材・パステル，水彩
用紙・画用紙

Method： Pastels, Water Colors
Paper： Drawing Paper

仕上り
Completed View

平面的に塗る
Evenly apply.

①

②パステルを別紙に塗り，擦筆につけて影になっている
　ところを濃く，明るいところは，むらをだしながら塗
　ります。

Apply the pastel to another piece of paper, and then onto a
stump. Shadows should be shown using a dark coat, and light
areas by applying the color unevenly.

③ボアになっているところは，細い擦筆に黒のパステル
　を付けソフトなタッチで描き入れます。

Use a thin stump in subtle touch with black pastel on it to
draw the boa.

擦筆で塗る
Use a stump.

②

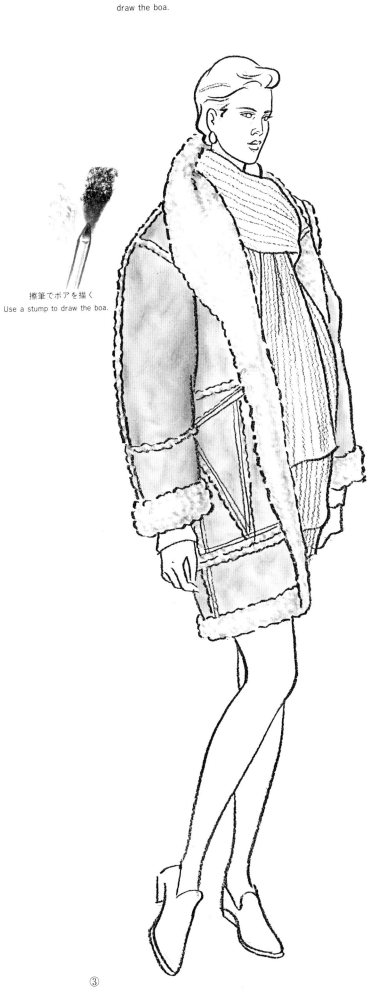

擦筆でボアを描く
Use a stump to draw the boa.

③

④水彩で，セーター，マフラー，タイツを塗ります。

Color in the sweater, scarf, and tights with water colors.

⑤ヘア・メークを色付けし，マフラーやタイツに編地を
入れて仕上りです。

Color the hair and make-up, and apply a knit pattern to the
scarf and tights to complete the illustration.

水彩で塗る
Use water colors.

水彩
Water colors

④

⑤

画材・パステル，色鉛筆
用紙・ケント紙

Method : Pastels, Colored Pencils
Paper : Kent Paper

仕上り
Completed View

① パステルをじかに省略的に塗ります。
Directly and partially apply pastels.

②指でのばしながら，ぼかします。
Spread the pastel with your finger.

練りゴムで光を入れる
Add luster with a paste eraser.

はみだしたところを消す
Erase any stray lines.

指でこする
Rub it in with your finger.

③

②

③光っているところを表現するために，練りゴムを角張らして消します。

Add luster using the corners of a paste eraser.

④一番光っているところは，色鉛筆の白で描き入れます。
Use a white pencil to show the brightest areas.

光を入れる
Add luster.

⑤

④

⑤シャツ，肌色，ヘア・メークを入れて仕上りです。
Add color to the shirt, skin, hair, and make-up to complete
the illustration.

レオパードの描き方 How to Draw Leopard-skin

画材・水彩
用紙・画用紙

Method: Water Colors
Paper: Drawing Paper

仕上り
Completed View

平面的に塗る
Apply evenly.

①

②同系色の濃い色で，斑点を入れます。
Draw the dots with a darker shade.

③黒に近いセピアの色で，斑点のまわりを不揃に囲みます。
Unevenly outline the dots with a very dark sepia.

斑点を入れる
Add dots.

斑点を囲む
Outline the dots.

②

③

④毛足を小筆で省略的に描き入れ，全体に濃いところは，
　太筆を使って濃く塗り，グラデーションにぼかします。

Roughly draw in the leopard-skin's hair with a small brush.
Use a dark color and a thick brush to color in the dark areas.
Add gradation.

⑤スカートや肌色，メークなどを入れて仕上りです。

Add color to the skirt, skin, and make-up to complete the
illustration.

毛足を描き入れる
Draw the hair.

濃いところを塗る
Color in the dark areas.

④

⑤

ミンクの描き方 How to Draw Mink

画材・ポスターカラー　Method : Poster Colors
用紙・画用紙　　　　Paper : Drawing Paper

①太筆で平面的に塗ります。
Evenly apply color with a thick brush.

仕上り
Completed View

①

②筆の毛先をバサバサにして色をつけ, 毛並みを描き込
みます。

Apply the poster color to a rather dry brush and draw the lie
of hair.

③細筆で濃さのめりはりをつけながら, 一本一本細かに
描き込んでいきます。

Carefully draw in each hair with a small brush, modulating
the darkness at the same time.

毛並みを描く
Draw in the lie of hair.

②

毛並みを一本
一本描き入れる
Carefully draw each hai

③

④細筆で明るいところの毛並みを、ホワイトで描き入れ
ます。中の洋服を塗ります。

Use a small brush and a white poster color to draw the hair
of the light areas. Color the clothes underneath.

⑤肌色やベルト，ヘア・メークを塗り仕上りです。

Color the skin, belt, hair, and make-up to complete the
illustration.

明るいところを描き入れる
Draw the light areas.

④

⑤

画用紙＋ボールペン＋水彩＋パントーン＋スクリーントーン
Drawing Paper＋Ball-point pen＋Water Colors＋Pantone＋Screen-tone

ケント紙＋サインペン＋ポスターカラー＋パントーン＋スクリーントーン
Kent paper＋Felt-Tip Pen＋Poster Colors＋Patone＋Screen-tone

画用紙＋サインペン＋水彩
Drawing Paper＋Felt-Tip Pen＋Water Colors

画用紙＋鉛筆＋クレヨン＋水彩
Drawing Paper＋Pencil＋Crayons＋Water Colors

画用紙＋ボールペン＋水彩
Drawing Paper＋Ball-Point Pen＋Water Colors

ケント紙＋鉛筆＋パステル
Kent Paper＋Pencil＋Pastels

画用紙＋鉛筆＋パステル
Drawing Paper＋Pencil＋Pastels

画用紙＋鉛筆＋パステル
Drawing Paper＋Pencil＋Pastels

画用紙＋色鉛筆＋パステル
Drawing Paper＋Colored Pencils＋Pastels

ケント紙＋筆ペン＋クレヨン＋水彩

Kent Paper + Brush-Pen + Crayons + Water Colors

ケント紙＋ダーマット＋クレヨン＋ポスターカラー

Kent Paper + Dermatograph + Crayons + Poster Colors

ケント紙＋筆ペン＋ポスターカラー＋マーカー

Kent Paper＋Brush-Pen＋Poster Colors＋Marker

画用紙＋サインペン＋筆ペン＋クレヨン＋水彩＋マーカー

Drawing Paper＋Felt-Tip Pen＋Brush-Pen＋Crayons＋Water Colors＋Marker

ケント紙＋竹ペン＋クレヨン＋ポスターカラー
Kent Paper + Bamboo Pen + Crayons + Poster Colors

ケント紙＋鉛筆＋ポスターカラー＋マーカー

Kent Paper＋Pencil＋Poster Colors＋Marker

ケント紙＋鉛筆＋ローソク＋ポスターカラー＋マーカー

Kent Paper＋Pencil＋Wax＋Poster Colors＋Marker

画用紙＋鉛筆＋マーカー

Drawing Paper＋Pencil＋Marker

画用紙＋サインペン＋マーカー

Drawing Paper＋Felt-Tip Pen＋Marker

画用紙＋サインペン＋マーカー
Drawing Paper＋Felt-Tip Pen＋Marker

画用紙＋竹ペン＋マーカー＋ポスターカラー

Drawing Paper＋Bamboo Pen＋Marker＋Poster Colors

ケント紙＋竹ペン＋マーカー

Kent Paper＋Bamboo Pen＋Marker

画用紙＋鉛筆＋マーカー
Drawing Paper + Pencil + Marker

ケント紙＋竹ペン＋マーカー
Kent Paper ＋ Bamboo Pen ＋ Marker

118

画用紙＋鉛筆＋水彩
Drawing Paper＋Pecil＋water Colors

ケント紙＋鉛筆＋クレヨン＋水彩
Kent paper ＋ Pecil＋Crayons＋Water Colors

ケント紙＋鉛筆＋クレヨン＋水彩

Kent Paper＋Pencil＋Crayons＋Water Colors

画用紙＋鉛筆＋水彩＋色鉛筆

Drawing Paper＋Pencil＋Water Colors＋Colored Pencils

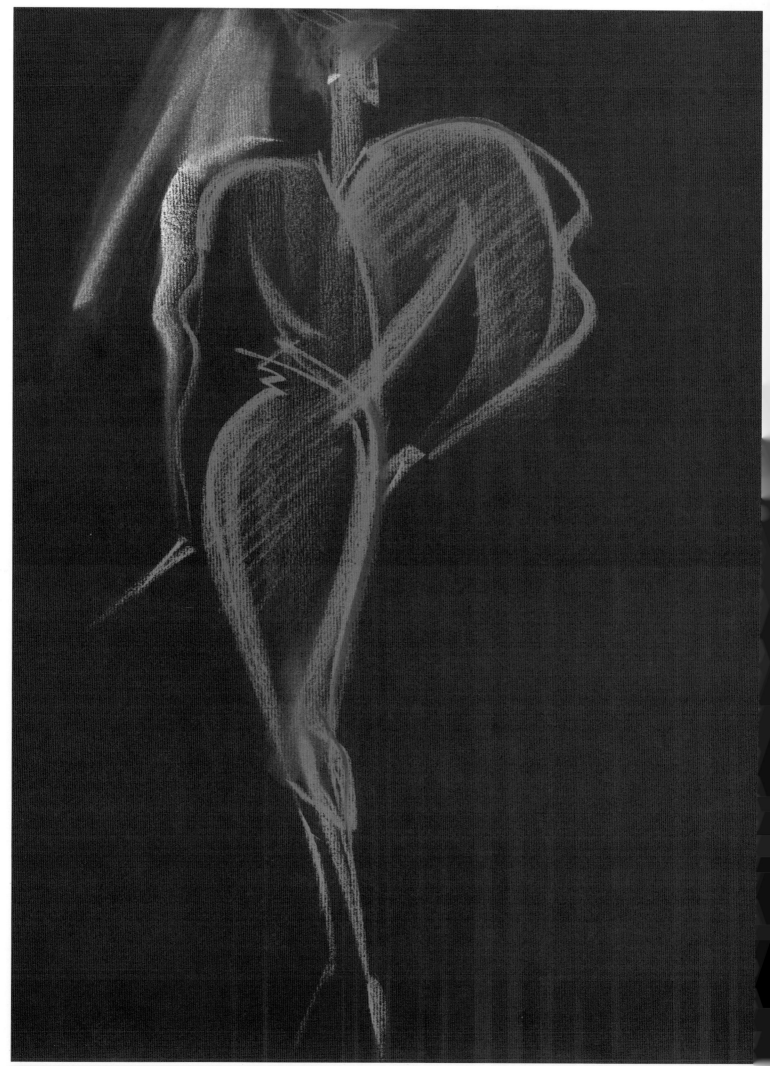

カラーコットン紙＋パステル　Colored Cotton Paper＋Pastels

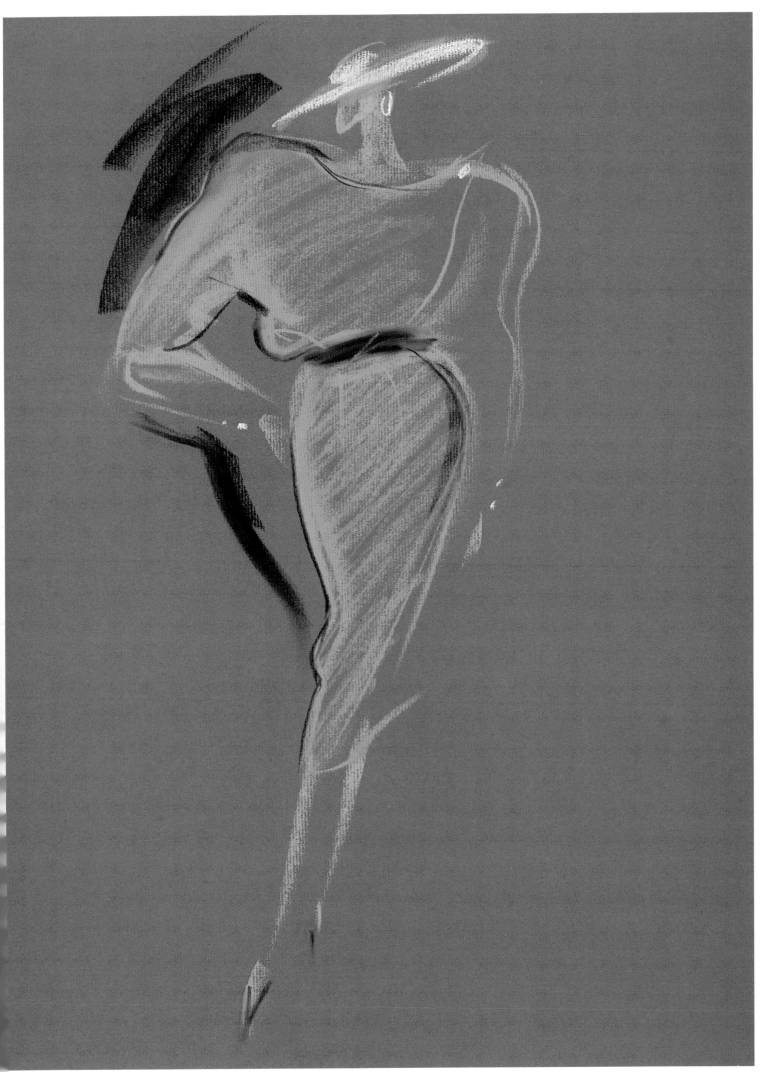

カラーコットン紙＋パステル　Colored Cotton Paper＋Pastels

カラーコットン紙＋パステル
Colored Cotton Paper＋Pastels

カラーコットン紙＋パステル
Colored Cotton Paper＋Pastels

プロフィール

1941年　山形県生まれ。

22歳の時に絵を描きたい一心で上京。デザイン学校でグラフィックの勉強。グラフィックの仕事についたが、自分の本当にやりたい仕事ではないと思い、自分の求めるものを模索している時に、スタイル画教室の広告が目に入り、ファッション イラストレーションを描くきっかけになり、そこで知り合った仲間達と SUN デザイン研究所を設立。1981年退社。

1981年　㈱アトリエ・フロム１を設立

1983年　熊谷小次郎イラスト教室設立

事務所　㈱アトリエ・フロム１

　　　　〒150 東京都渋谷区恵比寿西2-17-8

　　　　I. T. O. 代官山203号

　　　　TEL 03 (3464) 6048　FAX 03 (3464) 6052

PROFILE

Kojiro Kumagai

Born in Yamagata Prefecture, 1941. Came to Tokyo at the age of 22 to have some ambition for art in his mind. Studied graphic design and started as a graphic desiner. However, when he felt something different with it and had asked himself what he should do since then, he happened to know Masao Hara Drawing course. That was his turning point to fashion illustration. After that, he established Sun Design Laboratory with the friends of the Hara course. Resigned there in 1981, established his own office, "Atelier From One".

Head of Atelier From One.

Lectured in Kojiro Kumagai Illustration School.

Atelier From One; ＃203, I. T. O. Daikanyama, 2-17-8, Ebisu-Nishi, Shibuya-ku, Tokyo, 150

Tel. 03(3464)6048　Fax 03(3464)6052

ファッション イラストレーション2
素材の描き方

1988年6月25日	初版第1刷発行
1989年4月25日	第2刷発行
1990年3月25日	第3刷発行
1990年11月25日	第4刷発行
1991年11月25日	第5刷発行
1992年8月25日	第6刷発行
1994年1月15日	第7刷発行
1995年3月15日	第8刷発行
1996年3月15日	第9刷発行

著　者　熊谷小次郎（くまがいこじろう）©

発行者　久世　利郎

印　刷　錦明印刷株式会社
製　本　錦明印刷株式会社
写　植　三和写真工芸株式会社

発行所　株式会社グラフィック社
　　　　〒102 東京都千代田区九段北1-9-12
　　　　☎03(3263)4318　振替00130-6-114345

ISBN4-7661-0483-8 C3071

グラフィック社の好評図書

GRAPHIC-SHA BOOKS

スタイリングブック
FASHION WITH STYLE

高村是州著 by Zeshu Takamura
B5変型判・176頁 size : 257 x 190mm
pages : 176(80 in color)

マーカーで描く
ファッションイラストレーション
THE USE OF MARKERS IN FASHION ILLUSTRATIONS

高村是州著 by Zeshu Takamura
A4変型判・128頁 size : 300 x 225mm
pages : 120 (80in color)

ファッションルック
FASHION LOOK

柳沢元子著 by Motoko Yanagisawa
A4変型判・128頁 size : 300 x 225mm
pages : 128 (96 in color)

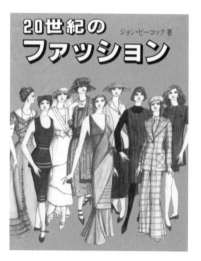

20世紀のファッション
20th–CENTURY FASHION

ジョン・ピーコック著 by John Peacock
A4変型判・240頁 size : 285 x 210mm
pages : 240 (144 in color)

西洋コスチューム大全
THE CHRONICLE OF WESTERN COSTUME

ジョン・ピーコック著 by John Peacock
A4変型判・224頁 size : 285 x 210mm
pages : 224(136 in color)

コスチューム ドローイング
COSTUME DRAWING

矢島 功+アトリエKO著 by Iso Yajima
A4変型判・144頁 size : 300 x 225
pages : 144 (96 in color)

ファッション イラストレーション
FASHION ILLUSTRATIONS

熊谷小次郎著 by Kojiro Kumagai
A4変型・144頁 size : 300 x 225
pages : 144 (40 in color)

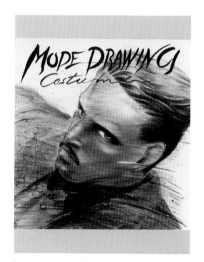

モード・ドローイング：コスチューム（男性）
MODE DRAWING : COSTUME(male)

矢島 功 著 by Isao Yajima
B4変形判・84頁 size : 268 x 255mm
pages : 84(24 in color)

カラースタイリング
COLOR WITH STYLE

ダーナ・フジイ著 by Donna Fujii
A4変型判・144頁 size : 300 x 225mm
pages : 144 (Full color)